BATTLES
OF THE HEART

BOOT CAMP For
MILITARY MOMS

Tracie Ciambotti

WESTBOW
PRESS
A DIVISION OF THOMAS NELSON

WestBow Press books may be ordered through booksellers or by contacting:

WestBow Press
A Division of Thomas Nelson
1663 Liberty Drive
Bloomington, IN 47403
www.westbowpress.com
1-(866) 928-1240

Author photo by: Beth Zitterbart, Photos By Design

Cover photo by: Carolyn Cummins, Shootin For Fun

Scripture taken from Zondervan NIV Study Bible (Fully Revised), Copyright 1985, 1995, 2002 by Zondervan. All rights reserved.

ISBN: 978-1-4497-3034-5 (hc)
ISBN: 978-1-4497-3033-8 (sc)
ISBN: 978-1-4497-3032-1 (e)

Library of Congress Control Number: 2011919643

Printed in the United States of America

WestBow Press rev. date: 1/27/2012

ENDORSEMENTS

"This is a brave, gripping story of what it is really like to be part of a military family. When a son, a brother, a husband, a daughter enlists to serve, their family enlists too. Tracie gives us a front row seat and walks us through the heartache and the courage of these families and the grace of God that shines in unexpected places."

Sheila Walsh, author of "God Loves Broken People...
and those who pretend they're not."

"In *Battles of the Heart* Tracie Ciambotti gives the reader a front row seat to her journey as the mother of a soldier in the U.S. Army. Her conversational style and willingness to share her feelings and emotions helps the reader to understand that supporting a loved one in the military is a continuing journey. I recommend her book to families who are starting their journey in any branch of the armed forces. You are not alone."

Dorie L. Griggs, M. Div.
Board Member, Care for the Troops

For

My mother, Dorothy Mae Zeller

and my grandsons,

Tristan Joshua Nearhoof
and Easton Tower Nearhoof

Contents

Part II: Boot Camp for Military Moms

FOREWORD

As a basic training chaplain, at graduations I hear our Battalion Commander tell the thousands of family members gathered in the sun and heat of Ft. Jackson, "Welcome to the Army family!" Nice words, but I have often thought, "They have little idea what they are getting into."

Indeed, I didn't join the military till I was the ripe old age of 34 and already married, with three children. Although I was "older and wiser" and had a father who was a retired Navy Reservist, my family and I didn't really know what we were getting into, either! *Battles of the Heart* is a refreshingly honest and needed testimony to some of the real-life emotional "trauma" that the family of a military service member encounters. Especially in this time of "persistent conflict" when our military heroes are often deployed in dangerous places, the family members left behind are the ones who truly have the harder job. Though everyone will respond differently, I believe you will find Tracie Ciambotti's personal account helpful in several areas as you deal with your loved one's enlistment in the military. Or you might find it useful in your being able to understand another who is struggling because their loved one now belongs to "Uncle Sam." The truth, which this book captures, is that there is a battle for your heart going on. The good news is that the God who made us and wants to have a personal relationship with us is the VICTOR, and through His grace and strength, we can overcome any obstacle or fear we face. Read on, ponder, pray, and connect with others in the same situation. You will be blessed if you do.

Chaplain (Major) Erik J. Gramling
Battalion Chaplain
1-61 Infantry Regiment
Basic Combat Training
Fort Jackson, SC

PREFACE

When my son, Josh, left on his first deployment to Iraq, I found myself in a very uncomfortable and frightening place. Prior to his training and deployment, I had no idea that his new life as a soldier would forever change mine. I was unaware of, unprepared for, and untrained to deal with the daily challenges that military families face. I didn't know that the family members—mothers, fathers, spouses, children, and siblings—all serve and sacrifice with the service member. No one told me that when my son went to war, I would be facing my own war at home.

The freedom that we, as Americans, enjoy every single day is not free; service members and their families pay a very real price for that freedom. I did not fully comprehend the cost of our freedom until my son enlisted in the Army and we became a military family.

Every military family has their own experiences; my story is only one of many. I want to share the incredible way in which God lavished His grace on me during my son's first deployment.

> As each one has received a special gift, employ it in serving
> one another as good stewards of the manifold grace of God.
> (1 Peter 4:10, *NIV Study Bible*)

This, then, is my attempt to be a good steward of God's grace by passing it on to every person who reads this book.

ACKNOWLEDGEMENTS

First, I thank my Lord and Savior Jesus Christ for His faithful presence in my life. I cannot imagine going through life's journey without Him.

Many thanks to the following individuals who helped make this book possible:

To my son, Joshua David Nearhoof and his wife, Alison Vergeront Nearhoof: Thank you both for allowing me to share your lives with the world.

To the members of the Christian Writers' Round Table of Central Pennsylvania: Thank you all for your constructive critique of my work. I have learned so much from this group.

To Laurel West, Director of the Christian Writer's Round Table:
I cannot begin to express my gratitude to you. First, for seeing something in me that I didn't know existed. Second, for believing in me and suggesting that I consider writing. You have been an encourager, a mentor, and a dear friend.

To my husband: Jeff, thank you for encouraging me throughout this project and for being my biggest fan.

To my daughters: Jessica and Danielle, I love you both more than you will ever know. You have grown into beautiful women, and you inspire me.

PART I

Battles of the Heart

INTRODUCTION

It is a quiet Saturday afternoon and my thoughts once again drift to my son. It has been six days since he left on his second deployment to Iraq and I have yet to receive word of his arrival. We spoke last Sunday, just hours before he reported to Fort Carson for departure. I told him how proud of him I am and what a wonderful young man he has become. I told him I loved him and would be praying for him every day. Then, fighting back the tears and forcing a strong voice, I told him to call when he could, but his first call should be to his wife. He said, "I know." We did not say good-bye, just "talk to you soon."

Having gone through one deployment, I feel mentally stronger and better prepared for what lies ahead. However, this time, when Josh is able to make a phone call, I know he will not be dialing my number. I am not an Army wife. I am an Army mom.

I tell my story for all the parents—and particularly, the moms—who have sons or daughters in any branch of our Armed Forces. I feel compelled to tell our war stories, expose our fears, and share our wounded hearts for our children. We are not part of the Family Readiness Groups and, for the most part, do not live close to the bases or posts where our children serve. We are scattered across the United States in rural areas, small towns, suburbs, and large cities. We represent every economic level, many races, and diverse religions. Yet, in essence, there is no disparity among us. We are moms of soldiers, airmen, sailors, marines, and Coast Guardsmen.

I will share my experiences and some tough lessons learned during my son's first deployment, and we will journey through his second deployment together. You may not encounter the same feelings and emotions that I did, as we are all different in that sense. But I hope that my story will expose some of the challenges of military life and prepare you to face your own situations with confidence.

Grab a cup of coffee, sit back and relax as we begin this journey together.

CHAPTER 1

When Did I Enlist?

HAVE YOU EVER thought, *Hey, wait one minute – did I miss the small print on the contract when my child enlisted? Where was the part informing me that when my child signs up, I am automatically enrolled to serve, as well?* This thought has crossed my mind many times.

Do you remember when your son or daughter first took you to the recruiter's station? What if the recruiter had handed you a brochure titled "Warnings—Just for Moms" and asked you to read it while your child was filling out the paperwork? Let's look at all the warnings it would have to include:

- Your child no longer belongs to you—he or she belongs to Uncle Sam.
- You cannot speak to your child during basic training unless he or she calls you.
- You will not see your child for extended periods of time.
- Your child's job is very dangerous and he or she could die.
- You will hear bad things on the news that will keep you awake at night.
- Your child, at times, may have to survive in horrendous living conditions.
- Your child is likely to see and do things that will haunt him for the rest of his life.

Imagine your response, as I share mine. I would grab my child, drag him out of the building, run to my car and probably get a speeding ticket on the way home. Then, I would lock him in his bedroom and forbid him ever to leave my sight again. Are you thinking the same thing?

I guess it is a good thing they don't have this brochure. After all, we do need service members, and who would ever let their children enroll if they knew all this upfront?

The fact is if you have a son or daughter in any branch of the Armed Forces, you are serving with them. There are differences in the ways we serve, but their commitment involves the entire family. They wear uniforms and we are in street clothes. They are trained and we are not. Other enlistees going through the exact same thing surround them; we are with the same family, friends, and co-workers as always. They are paid for their service but we are not.

I could go on and on here, but I think you get my point. We don't stop being moms when our children decide to serve their country. The commanding officer doesn't come pack our emotions up in a box, seal it with duct tape and confiscate it until the enlistment ends. They don't tell us what to expect or prepare us for our new role. In fact, they don't tell us that anything will change for us at all.

Our "mom emotions" keep flowing regardless of whom our child works for or where. I have news for you that the recruiter failed to mention. Your emotions are in for a ride, so buckle up.

CHAPTER 2

Moms: The Protectors

IT IS A MOTHER'S instinct to protect her children. From the moment we feel the first movement as they grow inside us, we take on the role of protector. It is our job to keep them safe and to teach them about avoiding danger. We are the ones who say, "Be careful; you'll get hurt." We are the caregivers, the ones who kiss their tears away and hug them until the hurts pass. It is a fundamental of motherhood.

Then they grow up and leave our nest. Some go off to college and some enter the work force. They can call home as often as they like. If they are close by, we see them frequently. We are the first ones they call when they get sick. "Mom, I have a sore throat. What should I take?" We get the call when they run out of money. "Mom, I'm broke. Can you transfer some cash into my account?" Our job is never finished. We are moms forever, no matter how old our children are.

However, when children join the military, the mother role we have played for eighteen years is suddenly ripped away from us. They are encouraged to write letters during basic training; phone calls, however, are not permitted. Calling home is a privilege they must earn. Time crawls by as we wait patiently at home.

Finally, we go to graduation. We are so proud to see our sons and daughters decked out in their spectacular dress uniforms. We are shocked to see their rooms spotless. We can actually see the floor and, WOW, their bed is not just made—you really can bounce a quarter off it. Someone else was able to achieve in 14 weeks (the length of my son's basic training) what we have attempted for the past 18 years. That someone else is our child's drill sergeant. Despite my being dubbed with this term a few times at home, now I understand the terror inflicted by the real deal.

After basic training, the recruits move on to their specialized training. That lasts another few weeks or so, depending on their specific military occupational specialty (MOS). Then we go to another graduation. At this point, we are in a bubble, completely inflated with pride for everything our child has accomplished. We pin special badges on the dress uniforms, take pictures, and celebrate.

Then come their "orders". Our new soldiers are assigned to their bases or posts, depending on the branch they serve in. Some report to their new locations and remain in the States. My son was assigned to Fort Hood, Texas and, within two weeks of arriving, was on his way to Baghdad, Iraq. That was the Monday after Thanksgiving, just five months after he graduated from high school.

What happens to our basic instinct to protect our child when he or she is ordered to one of the most dangerous places in the world? The one thing that comes so naturally to us, which we have done with ease for 18 years, is suddenly beyond our grasp. Oh, we still feel the need, but we are no longer able to protect our children! Worse than that, we cannot know exactly where they are, what they are doing, or if they are safe, injured or even alive. What now? How do we get through the day? How do we survive?

CHAPTER 3

Boot Camp–The Letters

THE DAY AFTER my son graduated from high school he was sworn into the Army and left immediately for boot camp at Fort Benning, Georgia. This part was not difficult for me, as I had already dealt with the issue of not having him around every day. Josh had decided at the age of fourteen to live with his father in Montana, which, to me in Pennsylvania, seemed like a world away. I had grown accustomed to being a long distance parent with weekly phone calls, short visits at Christmas, and extended visits in the summer. I was so proud of Josh for deciding to enlist in the Army. He hated school and the classroom setting. He loved being outside and was fascinated with guns and hunting; this was a good choice for him. I was eager to see what he would make of his new, structured environment.

My son wrote me ten letters while in boot camp. I saved every one. Aside from the fact that people rarely receive letters anymore, it is quite moving to read, word by word, what your child is going through, written in his own hand. I treasure Josh's letters and could probably write an entire book about them. But I will share with you the things that touched me most.

As I mentioned earlier, Josh hated school: reading, writing, math, anything that required him to sit still. The first letter I received made me chuckle. The envelope had no return address and did not have any name on it, just my street address, city, state and zip. I remember thinking, *That's my Josh.*

He began every letter with "Hey mom, it's me." He ended every one with "Love you" and signed his full name.

His first letter described a large reception center at Fort Benning where all new soldiers report for processing. This entailed, for starters, getting shots, company assignments, and uniforms. When he left for boot camp, he was instructed to take one change of clothes and one only. He wore blue jeans, a tee-shirt and his cowboy boots, the only pair of shoes he had with him.

Here is an excerpt from Josh's first letter explaining his initial few days:

> I'm sitting here at reception on day 3. Reception is a lot worse than I thought. Drill sergeants run it and it is real boring. Everywhere you go, you go in lines and formations. Yesterday we got our immunizations. We had to get 9 shots, 4 in each arm and one big penicillin in the left cheek. It's weird how everyone just falls together. There are probably 85 kids in this barracks and there are 41 kids in my company. They issued us our combat boots today and we got 2 pair of everything else. We've seen 1000 kids in and out of here the last 3 days. Some are still in civilian clothes that just got here, some are in physical training (PT) uniforms with their civilian shoes. Yeah, I've caught a lot of crap from the staff and the drill sergeant. I've had my black PT shorts on with my cowboy boots for the past 2 days.

At this point, I was laughing hard at the thought of Josh walking around for two days in shorts and cowboy boots. Even though he was not here, he was still making me laugh.

His second letter started out the same way:

> hey mom, it's me again, this is the second time I've wrote you, I hope you got the last one.

This letter opened my eyes to the extent to which discipline is applied to every minute of his day.

> The food is pretty good but you get no time to eat, you get about 5 minutes and if you look off your plate or talk, the drill sergeant makes you throw away what's left and leave.

The fourth letter was very special and really touched my heart.

hey mom, it's me. I got your letter, thanks for the card. It is Sunday the 26 of June it is 10:30. I just got back from church. I started going last Sunday. It's cool to go to church with a bunch of guys you are around 24/7. I have met lots of guys from everywhere and I get along with all of them. They have pretty good services at church. I found a motivating verse in the bible. They hand them out here, just the new testament though, they are pocket sized and camo on the covers. Anyway the verse is psalms 27:3: Though an army besiege me, my heart will not fear, though war break out against me, even then will I be confident.

The fact that Josh was going to church thrilled me. *And* he had quoted me a verse that spoke to him. Wow! It was like God was telling me "It's okay; I'm Josh's Protector now."

Each letter showed Josh's increased awareness that the world was bigger than just himself. It was evident that he was maturing daily.

The fifth letter was both exciting and sad. First, the exciting part:

We have finished red phase and have now entered white phase which means we have a lot more freedom. The drill sergeant picked a platoon guide and made me a squad leader, so I am in charge of 16 guys and have a lot of responsibility.

This confirmed to me that the Army was in fact a good choice for Josh. He'd found his place and was excelling. Now for the sad part:

It is now 8:00 pm and I just showered and am laying in bed. We got phone privileges earlier tonight. I called you and left a message, I don't know where you were, so I guess next time? Dad wasn't home either.

Talk about salt in a wound. The wound occurred the day he called, when I arrived home and listened to his message on the machine. My heart sank at the realization that I had missed his call—the first time he was allowed to phone, and I had missed it. The salt rub came when

I read this letter and was moved to tears because he was still thinking about not finding anyone home to talk to later that night when he wrote the letter. I was devastated!

The sixth letter awoke a new emotion in me.

> *Not to scare you or anything, but yesterday we were on the 300 yard range and we just finished our first fire generation. I was standing there along with every other guy in my platoon and all of a sudden a guy to my right, his shoulder jerked forward and he grabbed it and yelled hit. By this time you could hear whizzzz, zuvv and stuff. The drill sergeant yelled, "get down" and called an ALL range cease-fire and shut everything down. So turns out after the bullets stopped flying they took him out in an ambulance, the bullet came from so far away it just stuck in his shoulder about ¼ of an inch so he was fine. But still, talk about a scary time, I don't think I realized how serious it was till we were lying face down in the grass seeing the drill sergeant running down the line yelling get down.*

My son's words really pierced me. He hadn't realized how serious this particular situation was, and I certainly didn't think about how dangerous his new job could be until this letter. I did not dwell on it at this point, but the thought was never far from my mind.

His next letter made me so proud.

> *We just finished our 8 mile road march with our ruck sacks. The march is called highway to heaven, it is 5 miles of pretty flat, then the last 3 miles are really steep, we go back down, that is really hard for some. I am really good at ruck marches, so I was alongside my squad going up the last hill and this one guy in my squad was really sucking air and he wasn't going strong, so I told him to grab my ruck and I pretty much pulled him up the hill.*

Life wasn't just about him anymore; he was taking care of his guys. What a great feeling as a parent, to see your children giving it up for someone else.

The eighth letter was written just prior to a milestone for Josh.

Hey, it's me. It's Sunday the 24th of July. I turn 18 in 4 days, that's exciting. Somehow the drill sergeant found out about this so who knows what he has planned. I am getting very excited for family day, I can't wait to eat normally. I have not sat down to a meal and had more than 3 or 4 minutes to eat since I left home and therefore I forgot how to have a conversation while eating. The chow hall is always silent. The PX is just down the street so we'll have to go shopping there. I miss snacks like chips and candy and what I miss the most is drinking juice and soda. I have drunk nothing but water since I have been here. I forget what iced tea and soda taste like. Anyway, write soon, can't wait to see you.

As our scheduled visit drew closer, the last letter arrived.

Yesterday was the start of week 8, only 13 days till I see you. I am getting kind of excited to get a break from this place. I have been doing a lot of thinking about going to RIP Ranger program. I don't think I'm going to go . . . .

. . . I'm not dropping it because I don't think I can do it, I just don't want to be that high speed. As a ranger, I wouldn't have time for a family, as I would always be gone. Anyway just how I've been thinking, no final decisions yet. When you guys get here I will call my sergeant to see what my options are. Well, can't wait to see you.

For the first time, he was actually thinking about his future and how a decision today would impact his life down the road. It was very satisfying to see how he had matured. I was so anxious to see him, hug him, and tell him how very proud of him I was.

CHAPTER 4

Boot Camp—The First Visit

AT LAST, family weekend arrived and we could visit Josh. Imagine that: someone telling me I could visit my son! The Army had made it clear that he was no longer mine; he belonged to them.

We packed up our motor home, and my husband, Jeff, youngest daughter, Danielle, and I headed south. We stayed at a campground on post at Fort Benning. This was a new experience for me as I had never been on a military installation. Going through the security gates, obtaining a vehicle pass, having our motor home searched, and navigating our way around the post were all new. We settled in at our campsite, knowing we could not see Josh until the next day. It was a long evening for me as I waited to see my new soldier son the next day.

We went into town for a bite to eat and soon discovered that our trip to see Josh would produce many new adventures. Danielle, 15 at the time, begged us to go to a Sonics. I am not a fan of fast food, but because there is no Sonics in our hometown, I agreed. We pulled in and parked beside one of the menu boards, rolled down our window and perused our dinner options. Soon a young man on roller blades emerged from behind the vehicle to take our order. We learned a valuable lesson that night at dinner: Do not roll down your car windows at dusk, in Georgia, in the middle of August. Before long, our car was full of mosquitoes. For some reason, they all decided to feast on Danielle. Jeff and I did not suffer one bite between us, but she was covered with them. Her arms and legs were spattered with red marks that immediately turned into swollen, itchy masses. Our next stop was at a drug store to purchase some Benedryl.

The following morning we made our way to the designated area for families to report. A stern-looking man in uniform entered the room and introduced himself as our son's drill sergeant. He explained what his men had been doing the past six weeks and then gave us the dos and don'ts for the weekend. We would attend a ceremony, and then our soldiers would be released to us. We could not take them out of the Fort Benning area. They were not to drive a car or drink alcohol. They were to get plenty of rest, as going back to their rigid schedule after their first weekend of freedom was always a challenge. This was a very humbling experience for me. Aren't parents the ones supposed to be making the rules? Now someone else was laying out the conditions I had to abide by for a visit with my son.

We were directed to the next location, where the ceremony would take place, and waited anxiously for our soldiers to appear. Soon a sea of mottled green figures marched onto the field. They wore camouflage uniforms and beret hats. I later learned that they do not wear their dress uniforms for ceremonies during wartime. The ceremony was a fascinating display of parading soldiers performing special marches and following commands. I believe it is the Army's way of showing parents how they have turned our children into disciplined soldiers, who will respond immediately to any order. They lined up on the field and shouted out the Army creed. Finally, we were able to go onto the field and greet our new soldier. This was like picking out a particular spec of sand on a beach; they all looked the same. After diligent searching, we found Josh and he was ours for the weekend.

I immediately noticed a change in my son. You have to understand something about Josh: he is rarely serious about anything. As I've mentioned, Josh always makes me laugh. Even at those times when I had been screaming mad at him and threatening him with the punishment of his life, he would find a way to crack me up. His sisters always proclaim that Josh is my favorite because I could never get through a punishment without laughing. But today, he was serious. No artless grin, no teasing his sister or cracking jokes. He seemed broken. I guess that is what boot camp is all about: they have to break the soldiers down to retrain them.

Josh was required to wear his dress uniform in public. It was impeccable, his shirt freshly pressed and his slacks creased. Danielle was impressed with her big brother's shiny, spotless shoes. The contrast to his old jeans, tee-shirts and cowboy boots was astounding.

We were amazed, as well, when we went out to dinner. Every question our waitress asked Josh was answered, "Yes, Ma'am." We were shocked when he ate his vegetables and was the first one with an empty plate. I recalled from his letter that on post, he had five minutes to eat and was not allowed to talk or his plate would be tossed. So, even here with us, he ate and did not speak.

This visit brought mixed emotions. Part of me was thrilled and proud to see him so mature and disciplined. However, part of me was sad; the carefree Josh who was so much fun, the Josh we knew so well seemed to be gone, and I missed him.

CHAPTER 5

Prepare for Battle—Soldier and Mom

WHEN JOSH COMPLETED boot camp and his specialized training, he was assigned to Fort Hood, Texas. Within a few days of his arrival there, I received a phone call from his sergeant. He introduced himself and told me he was standing in the hallway outside Josh's room while Josh was inside doing pushups. He then asked me if Josh kept a messy room at home. Amused, I answered, "Yes." My smile broadened as I realized that the old Josh was not gone for good; when given a bit of freedom the real Josh had re-emerged. Later when I spoke to Josh, he said he could not believe it when his sergeant came into his room, said, "Oh, my God," and then told him to drop and start doing pushups. While he obeyed, the sergeant asked him for my phone number. Josh said he was thinking, *Are you serious? I'm in the Army, and you're going to call my mother because my room is a mess?*

The sergeant spoke cordially to me for quite some time. He asked if we were coming to see Josh for Thanksgiving and if we had heard about his new assignment.

Josh had been selected for a special mission because of his excellent marksmanship scores. He would join a private security detail whose sole function was to guard the life of the Deputy Division Commander. This group would be responsible for transporting the general wherever he needed to go. Josh would leave for Iraq the Monday after Thanksgiving.

Once again, we packed our motor home and headed south. Josh had a four-day pass for a long weekend, but he was not allowed to leave the area. We had a wonderful time, and it was so good to see Josh more like himself again. He seemed relaxed, joking around and picking on his little sister, which was always a good indication that he was okay.

He had to be back on post on Sunday, and saying goodbye was hard. I knew I had to be strong for his sake, but I was not feeling that way inside. I fought back tears as I reached to exchange that final hug, but I did not want to let go of him. I stretched up to give him a hard kiss on the cheek, and to whisper, "I love you and I'll be praying for you."

The trip home was a long one. I spent most of it in the back of our motor home alone. A million thoughts ran through my mind. My son was on his way to Baghdad as I headed for home. Boot camp had trained him well and he was ready for his mission. I, on the other hand, had no training. I was not prepared for all the emotions that were surfacing; in fact, I was completely unaware of the battle that lay ahead of me.

Once home, I went about my normal life. I was leading a women's Bible study group, and we were about eight weeks into Neil Anderson's study entitled, *Breaking through to Spiritual Maturity.* I had started as a co-leader when the group began in October, but the third week into the study, that changed. The leader stood at the end of the large conference table in the church library where we met. There were fourteen women seated around the long table as she began by telling the group that she had to go away for a while. Then she made eye contact with me and asked if I was prepared to take over as leader of the study. I cannot imagine the look that came over my face. My heart sank, and questions buffeted me. *Me, lead this group? How could I? I'm not a trained leader. I don't know enough. What if they ask questions I can't answer? What would I do?* I'm not sure how or why it happened, but my mouth opened and I said, "Yes." When I spoke to her later that evening, she shared that she was not sure why God was leading her elsewhere, but she felt very confident that it was God's plan for me to lead this study. I trusted her completely, so I embraced my new role, reasoning that if God had put me in it, He would provide what I needed. I did not yet know that God was preparing me for more than leadership of a Bible study group. He was preparing me for battle.

I wanted to keep up with current events in Iraq, so the TV was tuned to the news channel a lot. However, watching the news was suddenly different. It was not just information anymore: it was my life, and my son's life. More than that, without realizing it, I was marching right into battle with him. The difference was he knew where he was going and was fully dressed with protective armor. He had a helmet, bulletproof vest, M16, pistol, grenades. He knew who the enemy was and what to do. He was battle ready and trained to fight. I had no armor or weapons. I was completely exposed and unarmed. Worse yet, I didn't even know I had an enemy and had no clue what a battlefield looked like. Every time I heard of the mortal wounding of a US soldier, thoughts would flood my mind. *What if it was Josh? What if he's dead? What if he has lost a leg? What if they capture him and torture him, as they have done to others?*

Fear was becoming part of my every day, and sadness was right there with it. Each time I heard the news of more US soldier casualties, I found myself praying that it wouldn't be Josh; but then came the realization that it was somebody's son. My heart ached. Somewhere in the next day or so a mother would be getting a phone call or a knock at the door with the bad news. The grief was overwhelming. It was not long until I was paralyzed with fear. I dreaded the sound of the phone ringing, or the doorbell, for fear that my worst nightmare had come true. I was trying to be strong, to put on a tough front and hold it all in. The only thing that I accomplished was the building of a volcano inside me that was about to erupt. I remember going to my sister's house that year for our annual Christmas party. Having the whole family together except for Josh was hard enough, but everyone wanted to know how he was. I could barely speak without crying. Every time someone tried to talk to me, my eyes filled with tears and I thought the volcano raging in me would explode. It felt like someone was ripping my heart to shreds, one piece at a time.

I realized I was in crisis, but I didn't know what to do about it. I felt I had no control over what was happening to me, as if I were a victim. My emotions were completely driven by the news and events taking place on the other side of the world, and I couldn't change that.

I also felt like a failure. Here I was, leading a women's Bible study group, supposed to be an example of one having God in control of her life. But I didn't feel like anyone was in control, I felt as if my emotions and my life were spiraling off a cliff.

This was about the time when Baghdad was on the edge of civil war erupting right where Josh was serving. I prayed a lot and, feeling completely helpless to do anything else, sent an e-mail prayer request to my church's prayer chain. My request was for the protection and safety of my son in the midst of the horrifying events taking place in Baghdad. That e-mail was the beginning of a significant turn of events.

Our church has a Sunday evening Healing and Anointing Service. I don't go as regularly as I should but find myself going when I feel desperate, when there is nowhere else to turn. I went to this service the Sunday after I sent the e-mail. I could not bring myself to go forward to ask for prayer, so I sat in my seat and quietly cried out to God. The pastor's wife approached me after the service and said that she and the pastor had been praying for my son and me, and she felt God's leading to tell me that Josh was going to be okay. Wow! Just when I was about to raise my white flag and surrender to helplessness, God sent this dear messenger to tell me that He was watching over Josh.

For the first time in months, I felt a glimmer of peace in my heart, a tiny bit of hope, and the huge burden I was carrying started to feel a tinge lighter. I sat in my car after the service and wept. Slowly, through my tears, the volcano inside began to release its roiling heat. It was overwhelming and wonderful all at the same time. It seemed as the tears flowed out, the fear and sadness went with them, as if God were purging the negative, emptying me out so that He could fill me with His grace and mercy. Words escape me to describe this experience to you. If you have been the recipient of God's grace, you know exactly what I mean. If it has not yet come to you, my experience may seem incomprehensible. But, as amazing as this moment was, this was just the beginning of what God had planned for me. I had no idea what was still to come.

CHAPTER 6

A Meeting on the Battle Line

THE FOLLOWING MORNING, I began preparing for the next lesson our group would begin on Wednesday night. As I opened my study guide, I could not believe the title that stared back at me: "Winning the Battle for Your Mind."[1] I read the introduction to the lesson and tried to take in what was unfolding before my eyes. God was right there with me. He met me on the battle line with the weapons and ammunition I would need to survive. He had emptied me out the previous day, so there was plenty of room to store what He was about to give me.

The key verse for this session was 2 Corinthians 10:5:

> We demolish arguments and every pretension that sets itself
> up against the knowledge of God, and we take captive every
> thought to make it obedient to Christ.[2]

The knowledge of God's truth is the greatest weapon we can possess, and God provided that truth in this chapter of the study. I'd been completely ignorant of the fact that my mind was the point of entry for the battle raging within me. I didn't know that as a Christian, I actually had the power to control my mind and thereby control my emotions. I had no idea that Satan was the enemy and he was using the very information I was taking in from the news as his weapon against me to create fear.[3]

The next session in the study was entitled "Handle Your Emotions before They Manhandle You."[4] Isn't God amazing?

The key verse for this session was 1 Peter 5:7-8:

Cast all your anxiety on Him because he cares for you. Be
self-controlled and alert. Your enemy the devil prowls around
like a roaring lion looking for someone to devour.[5]

This chapter taught me how to let my mind control my emotions,
rather than letting my emotions and feelings dictate what I think.

When a thought enters our mind, we have a choice to make; of
course, we entertain it for a moment, but then we must decide whether
to hang on to it or disregard it. If we choose to hang on to it, then we
must choose what to do next. Do we act on the thought or just tuck
it away? I am certain each of us, at one time or another, has acted on
a thought that we probably should not have. You might think that as
long as you don't act on it, no harm will come from tucking it away.
Not true! Allowing that thought to remain in your mind is as good as
inviting Satan to use it. I fell prey to this trap. I heard a news report and,
yes, soldiers died. That did not necessarily mean that my son was one of
them, but because I allowed that thought to hang around in my mind,
Satan's tape recording began to play. *What if it was Josh?* Soon after I
started dwelling on those thoughts strong emotions emerged. Negative
thoughts will *always* cause negative emotions, and as women, we know
what happens when we have negative emotions, don't we? The battle
that began in the mind becomes a battle of the heart. The heart replays
and magnifies those negative feelings, and that tape recorder goes crazy.
That is where I was.

Let me share an excerpt from Neil Anderson's study guide. It really
speaks truth to this situation.

> You are not shaped as much by your environment as you
> are by your perception of your environment. Life's events
> don't determine who you are; God determines who you are,
> and your interpretation of life's events determines how well
> you will handle the pressures of life.
>
> We are tempted to say, "He made me so mad!" or "I wasn't
> depressed until she showed up!" That's like saying, "I have no
> control over my emotions or my will." In reality we have very
> little control over our emotions, but we do have control over
> our thoughts, and our thoughts determine our feelings and
> our responses. That's why it is so important that you fill your

mind with the knowledge of God and His Word. You need to see life from God's perspective and respond accordingly.[6]

Think about the last time you and your hubby had a disagreement. Did you resolve it on the spot, or did one of you leave the room angry? I will admit that I usually leave the room angry. Then I go to my bedroom, and thoughts start swimming around in my head: *I can't believe him. What a jerk. He always does this. This is exactly what he did the last time we fought. He just doesn't understand anything. What do I have to do, spell it out for him?* Do any of these thoughts sound familiar to you? Where do these thoughts come from? With spontaneity, they show up every time I fight with my spouse. I experience an entirely different set of thoughts when the disagreement is with one of my kids. In fact, there is probably a different set of thoughts for each kid. Do you get what I am saying here? These thoughts arise because, in each case, I have chosen to keep them, and Satan loves it when we do that. Imagine his satisfaction each time he pushes the "play" button on that tape recorder and we fall into the same trap we have been in a hundred times before. Each entrapment for him is more thrilling than the last.

I'd like you to try something that I found to be quite helpful in stopping this cycle. Once I understood where these thoughts were coming from, it was easy to recognize them when they first showed up, and so, I would simply command them to stop. It worked, and it continues to work. I am not kidding you; sometimes I go and stand in front of my mirror, look myself in the eye and say, *"Enough . . . stop it, now!"* It is amazing; you can actually force thoughts out of your mind. Try it. Learn to capture negative thoughts as they enter your mind, before they can take root, sprout into fear and take control of your heart and emotions.

Through Neil Anderson's Bible study, God supplied everything I needed to win my battle. I'm not going to tell you this was easy; in fact, I'm going to admit it was very hard. I had to work at this every day to break old habits and patterns and create new ones. I spent a lot of time pouring my heart out to God and asking for strength to continue. I searched my Bible, found new truths, and added more ammunition. As I studied a passage in 1 Peter, the verses clearly spoke to me. "Humble yourselves, therefore, under God's mighty hand, that he may lift you up in due time" (1 Peter 5:6, *NIV Study Bible*).

I needed to humble myself before God first, so He could lift me up. Verse 10 says: "And the God of all grace, who called you to his eternal glory in Christ, after you have suffered a little while, will Himself restore you and make you strong, firm and steadfast" (1 Peter 5:10 *NIV Study Bible*).

I did suffer a little while, and God did restore me; I did emerge stronger in faith, firm in His truth and with my focus steadfast on Him. That verse became one of my favorites and the inspiration for this poem:

I sit on a sandy beach in the quiet of the dawn
Waves gently meet the shore, whispering peace, bringing calm
The sun climbs the horizon; bright colors fill the sky
The beauty overwhelms me; tears slip from my eyes
Today the waves are tranquil; yesterday there was a storm
In its fury I was tossed around; I'd been battered and worn
But wait, in the distance a great vessel I see
Mighty in size, yet the crew is only three
God is the captain; He's sailing toward me
He's showering me with grace to cover my need
Jesus is the lifeline dangling from each side
Offering a safe place, an anchor for my life
The Holy Spirit waits patiently for me to come on board
Then in His mercy fills me till I hunger and thirst no more
This mighty ship has come to me with everything I need
I fall to my knees before my King. At last I am free!

Breaking through to Spiritual Maturity was an incredible study, and I am amazed every time I think about how God placed me in it at the time of my son's first deployment. Throughout this study, Anderson presents a true picture of God's grace and provision for our lives. God knew that my son would be going to Iraq and that I would fall apart. I had no idea why the Lord led me to this study or why He called me, early on, to lead it. At that time, Josh was still in training in the States and I had no clue where he would go upon finishing. I believe God opened the door for me to lead the study because He wanted me completely focused on its crucial and timely truth. He wanted to teach me how to apply the truth first to *my* life and then use that as an example to the women in my group. I have participated in other studies and learned from them, but leading a study requires one to put so much more into it. I spent a lot of time in prayer, reading and rereading the material, and looking up related verses. This study was a turning point in my life and without question raised me to a new level of spiritual maturity.

CHAPTER 7

The Tour Continues—His and Mine

AS JOSH'S TOUR in Iraq continued, my spiritual journey was taking me to new places.

My Bible study group moved into the second part of *Breaking through to Spiritual Maturity,* and I was discovering new truths and growing stronger with each one. The final lesson, entitled "Taking Steps to Freedom in Christ"[7], guided me through seven steps to achieve personal freedom in the Lord.

The key verse for this session was Galatians 5:1: "It is for freedom that Christ has set us free. Stand firm, then, and do not let yourselves be burdened again by a yoke of slavery."[8]

The key idea was; "Our daily victory in Christ is tenuous at best if we fail to do our part in laying hold of our freedom."[9]

I wanted that daily victory and needed to do my part to achieve it. This was difficult and painful but worthwhile. I was able to come to terms with hurts, sins, and unresolved issues from my past, some of which I did not realize I had tucked away, deep inside.

I won't go into all of these, but I do want to share one area. I had been hanging on to guilt over my decision, many years ago, to end my first marriage in divorce. When you hold on to negative feelings of any kind, they create an opening for trouble to creep in. Suppressing hurt, doubts, or guilt does not necessarily influence every moment but does affect the way you respond to certain situations. I had confessed and received forgiveness from God for my part in allowing my marriage to fail. However, I had not confessed to and asked forgiveness from those

I had hurt, and I had not forgiven myself. This process can be quite painful because it requires one to dig up the past, relive the hurts, and face those involved. Once you open those old wounds, the feelings flood in. It's like a dam breaking and allowing the storm water to crash into you. The study warned me to stay very close to God during this process, as allowing these old feelings to surface can become confusing and overwhelming. The goal was to resurrect the feelings, ask forgiveness, and then let them go. The key to success with this is releasing any expectation that the person you are asking for forgiveness will actually forgive you. You cannot control how that person will respond, so you have to be prepared for all possibilities. His or her forgiveness is helpful and certainly makes you feel better, but is not necessary for your healing. This is very difficult for me because I plan my conversations, including what I perceive to be the correct response of the person to whom I am speaking. (How dare someone not respond according to my plan!) This falls under the "faulty thinking" chapter of the study, which I obviously have not yet mastered.

With this in mind, I tackled the task, starting with my daughters. I spoke to each, individually, and told her I was sorry for how my decision to end my marriage to their father had affected her life forever. The girls' experiences from the divorce were very different; the older was 12 at the time, the younger, only two. Both girls were very gracious. Of course, they had questions, which developed into good conversations. These intimate talks brought a sense of peace to me.

I spoke to Josh when he was home for his mid-tour leave. Jeff, Danielle, and I had traveled to Montana for this visit so Josh could spend time with both his father and us. This was a very emotional conversation as it was the first time I had seen Josh since he had left for Iraq, and strong emotion was inherent in that alone. Add to that my apologies for my divorce, and I babbled and bawled through the entire exchange. Fortunately, Josh listened intently, his eyes searching my face; I felt sure he was wondering if I had finally lost it and was ready for a straight jacket. I recall his saying, "Mom, it's okay" over and over again as his girlfriend, Alison, patiently waited in the car.

I was just about done with this process, but there was one person remaining to whom I needed to apologize—my ex-husband. I expected this to be the most difficult conversation, and it was. However, it brought freedom from the guilt I had carried all those years, and I was finally able to forgive myself. Isn't it true that often we don't realize how heavy our burdens are until we needn't carry them anymore? What marvelous release I experienced that day! And with it came a new level of spiritual maturity that I didn't know existed.

We savored every moment we had with Josh in Montana. Soon he was on a plane heading back to Iraq for the second half of his deployment. He called every few weeks throughout this deployment. It was always a relief to hear his voice. There were things he would tell his dad that he did not tell me—which I've come to learn is a good thing. I just don't need to know everything that is going on when he is at war.

The function of Josh's unit, as I mentioned previously, was to transport and protect the Division Commander. This commander was required to go to every location where an attack on US soldiers occurred. He would have to inspect the site and write a report on the incident. One such incident took the lives of several soldiers. I remember Josh's telling of his unit's arrival on the scene of this tragedy. The survivors of the targeted unit were picking up the remains of their fellow soldiers who had died. Josh said he and his unit immediately went to them and offered to do this horrible task. They did not feel it was right for these soldiers to have to perform this duty for their own men. I was astonished at the amount of bravery it took to offer to do such a grisly job. I was also heartbroken over what my son had seen and what he'd had to do. He told me he was having nightmares and couldn't get those images out of his head. The men were instructed by their commanding officer to meet with a counselor after such a traumatic event. I encouraged Josh to do that and not be too proud to ask for help.

Josh's unit did have one narrow escape (the only one that I know of). They were out on their daily mission when the second truck in their convoy of four vehicles hit an IED (improvised explosive devise). The blast rendered the vehicle immobile.

A tactic used by the insurgents was to disable the first vehicle, which would then stop the ones behind it. When everyone emerged from their vehicles, the insurgents—conspicuously located on nearby rooftops—would begin to fire on the soldiers. The standard procedure was to remain inside the vehicles and the second truck in the group would then move forward and push the disabled one out of the danger zone.

In this particular situation, the second vehicle was the one that hit the IED and could not be pushed due to its total destruction. The only option was for the lead truck to tow the disabled one. As the soldiers dismounted the vehicle and conducted recovery operations they came under intermittent gunfire from the convoy's three o'clock position, however the exact location of the gunfire was unknown. As the vehicle gunners scanned their sectors for possible enemy firing positions, the soldiers who were on the ground continued to hook up the vehicle tow bar. Once it was secured the unit egressed and returned to their base.

Fortunately, only one soldier sustained a minor injury during this incident; a piece of shrapnel, had lodged in his foot.

Josh's deployment ended in November, and he returned to his home post at Fort Hood, Texas. Once again, we made the long trip south. We picked him up at Fort Hood and traveled to San Antonio, where we spent a long weekend. I have come to treasure the time I get to spend with Josh. There is no worry or fear for his safety when he is with me. We take this for granted with our other children, who are not service members. We never think of our time with them as "limited", but that thought is never far away when I'm with Josh. I never know when or if I will see him again; hence I cherish every moment.

Josh and Alison were married in December of 2006, but the formal ceremony would have to wait. When you are serving in the military, you can't just schedule vacation time for events in your life. You are told when you are allowed to take leave, and you must squeeze as much in during that time as possible.

Josh remained stationed at Fort Hood, Texas until May of 2007, when his unit relocated to Fort Carson, Colorado.

In August of 2007, we traveled to Polson, Montana for the long awaited wedding celebration. This trip included my husband, Jeff, older daughter, Jessica, younger daughter, Danielle, and my mother, Dottie. It was a breathtaking outdoor ceremony at Josh's new in-laws' ranch. Seeing Josh in his Army dress uniform instantly brought tears to my eyes. I fondly remember the proud moments I spent with him at the reception as we danced the mother-son dance.

As I reflect on those first two years after Josh joined the Army, it is easy to see how both my son and I have changed. We have grown in diverse ways; we are different people because of the military experiences we have had. His experiences caused him to mature quickly into a physically strong, independent, and responsible young man. My experiences caused me to grow spiritually closer to my Lord and Savior, to become wholly dependent on Him and not rely on my own understanding or abilities. Ironically, Josh was trained by the Army to be self-sufficient, and the Lord taught me the exact opposite. We have both learned the value of obedience.

As we journey through the next deployment together, I wonder how many more lessons we will learn from the experiences yet to unfold.

CHAPTER 8

Prisoners of the Phone

IT IS SUNDAY afternoon, and I am fast asleep in my family room recliner (my weekly nap ritual). My cell phone, on the table beside me, rings and awakens me. I grab it, trying to shake off drowsiness. It is an odd number starting with 999, obviously not anyone in my contact list. I flip it open and say, "Hello."

"Hellllooo," he answers, just the way he always does. The long awaited call has come; for the first time since he left for his second Iraq deployment over three weeks ago, I hear my son's voice.

The mom of a soldier is a prisoner of her phone. My cell phone is close to my hand at all times, and I mean *all* times. I do not move without my phone. Wherever I go—to play golf, take in a football game—it is with me. When I'm in the car, I keep it in my hand or lap so I do not miss the ring as I listen to the radio. I put it on "vibrate" when I'm in church, Sunday school or my weekly Bible study meeting. It is on my nightstand when I sleep, on my desk while I work, on the counter while I cook, on the washer while I switch laundry, and in the bathroom with me regardless of the reason I am there. This may seem a bit obsessive to some, but seasoned moms of soldiers will agree, you can't risk missing a phone call. You never know how long it will be until the next one comes. At the end of every call, the same thought haunts you: *What if I never speak to him again?* Nothing can break your heart more than missing a call, knowing it might be his last.

What happens, for me, when the call finally comes? It's as if I instantly morph into someone else. I'm fighting back emotions daily, I wait and wait and wait, and then finally, when he calls, I just melt. All the feelings I've been suppressing start to bubble up, and now I take a deep breath to cork them just a bit longer until the call ends. Conflicting emotions compete for my attention. The fear melts, as I know he is okay, at least for now. I am so happy to hear his voice I cling to every word. The mom in me tries to analyze the tone of his voice—does it sound just right? My limited time to talk turns into an inquisition, as I must have every single detail, so I fire off my questions. How are you? What time do you get up? What time do you go to bed? What do you do all day? What did you eat today! The list of questions is endless and many more run through my mind, but I don't dare ask for fear of hearing something that may keep me awake at night.

I try to be very careful not to go overboard, but it is hard. As much as I need information, I do not want his call to be a grueling interrogation for him. Sometimes, I have to force myself just to listen to him talk and not be a private investigator. Then I tell him what is going on here; he needs a sense of security that everything back home is fine. Even if things were falling apart here, I would never burden him with that. He cannot afford any distractions; he must be completely focused on his job. That is a matter of life or death.

When this call came, I knew immediately that Josh's voice was different. Upon arrival in Kuwait, he had come down with a virus, which is a common occurrence for the men. Most deployments begin with a few weeks in a safe place to get through the acclimation period. The soldiers' bodies have to adjust to a very different climate, and their resistance to illness is challenged. Since they live in such close quarters, when one gets sick, they all get sick. Josh was recovering from an upper respiratory infection.

Josh described the base in Kuwait as a large, very well equipped post, much like a small city. He said they would be there a few more days and would then head into northern Iraq, where he would spend the next twelve months. His brigade would divide into companies and go to different locations. His company, about 130 soldiers, would be going to a COP (combat outpost). This small post, located about forty miles away from the main post, would lack basic living amenities. The food and water would come in weekly from the main base. There would be no laundry facilities; they would have to wash their clothes in the shower. They could send their clothes to the main post to be laundered but would not get it back for ten days. They would have to burn their bodily excrement and would actually be showering in salt water. There would be no PX (store) on the post, so they would not be able to purchase basic items like toothpaste, body wash, shampoo, and shaving cream.

I was completely shocked and angry at the deplorable living conditions my son would call home for the next year. I told him I would send him anything he needed to make this time more bearable. This tour was certainly shaping up to be different from his first tour, with a new set of emotions on the verge of erupting from me.

The call ended with the standard "I love you. I'm praying for you. Take care, and call when you can." The minute I hung up the phone, the dam broke and the surge of emotions swept me to the breaking point. I left the room and went away by myself to allow the flood to take its course. Experience has taught me to let the emotions flow out of me, because trying to contain them is a recipe for disaster. I learned that lesson during Josh's first deployment. When the flood of emotion subsides, I am quiet once again. I spend some time alone with my Savior. I cry out to God to watch over and protect my son. I ask Him to help Josh focus on his job and not get depressed with the living conditions he is facing. I pray for strength to deal with the emotions this next year will bring. I ask God to pour His grace and mercy upon me as I embark on this new journey.

> Consider it pure joy, my brothers, whenever you face trials
> of many kinds, because you know that the testing of your
> faith develops perseverance. Perseverance must finish its
> work so that you may be mature and complete, not lacking
> anything. (James 1:2-4, *NIV Study Bible*)

I read and absorb these words and find solace in their truth. I know that God will teach me new things during this time; my head is on board with that. My heart is what I have to force along for the ride. That is hard. Whenever I struggle to get my heart where my head is, I've found that worship music helps tremendously. It lifts the heaviness.

I attended a Women of Faith conference this past summer in Washington, DC. The theme was grace. How appropriate that God planted me there, knowing that I would need a generous supply of it over the next year. The worship team was amazing. I purchased their CD, and the chorus of one of the songs on it spoke deeply to me. Let me share it with you. I pray these words will penetrate your heart as you read them. The song, entitled "Rescue", was written by Jared Anderson.[10]

> I need you, Jesus, to come to my rescue.
> Where else could I go?
> There's no other name by which I am saved.
> Capture me with grace, I will follow You.

This chorus has become my plea to God. When my heart is heavy and I can't seem to get it moving, I cry out these words to God. They have become my bedtime prayer, I sing them in the shower, and I often have the CD playing while I'm working. God meets me during these times and covers me with His grace, lifting my heavy heart and filling it with a sense of peace.

> Yet the Lord longs to be gracious to you; He rises to show
> you compassion. For the Lord is a God of justice. Blessed are
> all who wait for Him! (Isaiah 30:18, *NIV*)

It amazes me when the truth of God's word touches me. He longs to be gracious to us; all we have to do is humbly wait for Him.

CHAPTER 9

The Battle Goes On

I HAVE COME to accept that as long as I am an Army mom, this battle will go on. When soldiers return home from deployments, they rest, reconnect with their family and immediately begin training for the next mission. When Josh is in the States, things are calm and I rest. When he is on deployments, I gather my battle gear and prepare for a new fight. I've heard the saying that peace is not the absence of war; it is the ability to remain calm in the midst of it. Military life is a hard life for the soldier and his family. The soldier's hard time is obvious when he is deployed: he is away from family and friends for extended periods, endures unbearable living conditions at times, sees and does things that may haunt him for life, and risks his life daily. The family's hardship during a deployment looks different. Wives deal with loneliness and having to run households alone. We all, including the extended family, deal with sadness from missing him, fear for his life, and the harsh reality that we don't know where he is or what he is doing most of the time. What I choose to do with these hardships will determine my success or failure at finding peace.

At this writing, Josh's unit has just transferred to Mosul, Iraq. The living conditions there are like those at a Marriot Resort compared with the last location, near Kirkuk, so that is good news. Unfortunately, Mosul is one of last areas in Iraq that Sunni terrorists are holding onto. Earlier this week, I saw a news item scrolling across the bottom of the screen reporting that four US soldiers were killed in Mosul. My heart sank and I immediately went to the Internet for details. Josh had just arrived at this location, and soldiers are now dead. The fear for his life that paralyzed me during his first tour in Baghdad reached out to grab hold of me once more. *Will I worry day and night over his safety, again?* I asked myself. *No, I will not!* I vowed, and knew immediately what to do. I asked God to clear my mind of those thoughts that were nothing but a trap for me—a trap I would not fall into again.

The key to my daily success is making good choices. As I've said, I cannot avoid every uncomfortable circumstance, but I can decide how to respond to each. It is my choice and I do possess the power to deal with the situation wisely. The question is, will I?

This deployment seems to be bringing plenty of opportunities to test this. One thing I have struggled with is the lack of communication. Josh was not married during his first deployment, so when he was able to call, he would call me, and his father. This time, when he is able, he phones his wife – which he should. However, the mom in me longs to hear his voice and tends to allow jealousy to creep in. After all, I was his mother before she was his wife. It's hard when you know in your head the right thing to do, but your heart and feelings still crave what you think you deserve. I have to force myself repeatedly to capture and extinguish those thoughts quickly.

Because I've stayed in close contact with my daughter-in-law, Alison, I realized early into this deployment that she was in unfamiliar territory herself. She was a new bride and her husband was gone—for a year. She missed him terribly. It occurred to me that when you start feeling sorry for yourself, you need to look around; you don't have to look far to find someone struggling more than you are. I decided to focus on her, try to be supportive and offer encouragement whenever I could, rather than allow negative feelings to take root. This is a constant effort, as each new situation that arises must be handled, and often we must get refocused.

I was informed in January that I would not be seeing my son on his mid-tour leave in March. I was devastated! Anger flared and then melted into hurt. Then, my mind went crazy with the "what ifs". *What if I don't see him during mid-tour and then something happens to him? How would I live with that?* I needed to talk this over with Josh, but because I couldn't call him, I sent an e-mail. He responded that he and Alison really needed to spend the time together, alone. I completely understood their need, but the mom in me was crying out, *What about my need to see my son?* I replied that I did not agree with his decision, but I would respect his wishes. I didn't want him to be worrying about this when he needed to be focused on his job and keeping safe.

I knew these feelings of hurt and anger would lead to bitterness and resentment, so I did the only thing I could do—I prayed. I asked God to pour His grace on me as He had done so many times in the past and to give me the ability to accept this and find peace with it. He did! It took time and daily prayer, but God took those feelings away.

As the mid-tour leave got closer, though, the feelings started creeping back in. Alison was getting so excited that it was almost time for Josh to come home, which I completely understood. But it was very hard to be happy for her when I wanted to see him just as badly but was not allowed. I found myself angry and jealous all over again. I decided I would discuss this with Josh again when he arrived in the States. I did not want to make a big deal of it or fight about it, but I needed to tell him this was not right. I asked the women in my Bible study group to pray for wisdom: that God would let me know the right time to initiate this conversation and give me the right words. I prayed about this myself for weeks leading up to Josh's arrival in the States. Guess what. I did not find a "right" time to have the conversation. Josh called many times during his leave and I didn't feel any need to bring it up. In fact, it was clear to me that I was not to bring it up. God spoke clearly, took away the negative feelings, and gave me peace. I'm learning that when you ask God for wisdom in a particular situation, you must be obedient to His leading, even if He leads you where you did not expect to go. I started this situation with strong feelings that I was right and had every reason to feel hurt. I was asking God to help me speak the truth to my son and to do so with love. Instead, God showed me that I was wrong. I had allowed emotions and feelings to control my thoughts instead of having correct thinking control my feelings.

Josh's mid-tour leave ended and he was on his way back to Iraq. Alison called to tell me that five US soldiers from his unit were killed in Mosul—young men he knew. Josh was aware of this incident but did not know who had died in the attack. It was heart breaking to me. He had just finished a three-week rest in the middle of a yearlong tour. He was refueled and ready to serve out the deployment. Upon his arrival, he would learn who the fallen soldiers were, and that would start the second half of his tour. Think about returning from your vacation to find out that several of your co-workers have died. I cannot fathom how soldiers can process and accept this devastating news and then just continue. I was saddened, obviously, by the loss of life itself, but also that my son had to begin the second half of his tour this way.

I've learned and accepted that life is not fair and things do not always work out the way we want them to, or the way we think they should. Military life in particular is not fair. There are many sacrifices made by both the soldier and his family. The entire family serves right along with their soldier, but without the benefit of the training and preparation. Family members have to figure out how to survive the battle once they find themselves smack in the middle of it.

As a Christian, I am so thankful that God continues to provide me with everything I need to be successful during this time. I've grown to understand that my daily success does not depend on my perfection, as that would be impossible. It depends on my persistence in seeking God's will in all things.

CHAPTER 10

Sneak Attack

CONTROL OF IRAQ'S security has just been handed over to their government. American forces have pulled out of most cities and outposts. There are no more missions or raids; our soldiers are just sitting around on the American bases in case a need arises. This is a happy day for me. The risk of something going wrong on a fully populated post is slim, and I feel it's smooth sailing from here on out. Soon, this tour will be over and my son will be back on American soil.

Do you remember when your kids were young and suddenly everything was quiet? It usually meant they were into something they should not have been. Mothers of toddlers always have to be on alert. Guess what. The same rule applies when you are a military mom. Just about the time you let down your guard and think all is calm, the door swings wide open to a sneak attack.

Josh's unit was scheduled to arrive back at Fort Carson in Colorado in mid-August. By this time, I was very anxious to see him; it had been a long year. I started planning (in my mind anyway) to make the trip to Fort Carson, to be there when he arrived. I was in awe of the thought of participating in the welcome home ceremonies on post.

However, much to my dismay, once I announced my plans to my son and daughter-in-law, I was asked not to come for the ceremony but to arrive the following weekend. That was not possible because my younger daughter was to start college the following Monday. The reasons Josh and Alison gave were good: the date was a moving target; there could be flight delays; there are a million things to do those first couple of days back, and so on. My emotions once again moved into the "control" position and all I heard was, "You are not allowed to see your son"—again. I was crushed. I took the closed door very personally, feeling I no longer mattered to Josh. I kept thinking, *Don't they understand that I'm his* mother? *I have a right to see my son. I respected their wishes for mid-tour leave, and now I'm desperate to see him, to hug him, to just make sure he's okay.*

I got into a discussion about this with Alison one night during a Facebook chat. For future reference, I don't recommend this. Once you allow your emotions to slip into the driver's seat, they will take you places you don't want to go; you will say things you don't want to say—and I did. I vented when I should not have and I made my daughter-in-law feel horrible. As she desperately urged me to see her side, I tried harder to persuade her to see mine. There were no winners here. I could not understand how she felt: I've never been married to a soldier. She could not understand how I felt: she was not yet a mother. We were both fighting for the same thing—we just wanted time with Josh—but we were fighting from opposite sides. She said that the next time she spoke to Josh she would ask him to call me. I told her not to, as I didn't want him to worry about this right now. It was fine; we just would not come.

The following day, I was on my way to the annual Women of Faith conference in Washington, DC. I was with my daughter Danielle, my sister, Terri, and my mother, Dottie. We were nearing the church where we would board the bus for the trip to DC, when my cell phone rang. The caller ID was a bizarre number and I knew instinctively that it was Josh. My heart sank. I answered the call and we exchanged the usual pleasantries. Josh proceeded into the conversation I was dreading. As I listened to him, my heart broke one piece at a time. He said it was so hard for him and Alison to know what to do. They were trying to make a life together, make mutual decisions, do all those things young couples have to do to stay close. But it was extremely complicated when the military controlled your life, told you what you could do and when, and limited your time off. He said he felt guilty about not seeing me on his mid-tour leave, and telling me now to wait a bit longer made him feel worse. He told me he was worried that I was going to be mad at him and never want to speak to him again. I was now fighting the tears as they slipped from my eyes. He said, "Mom, I'm trying to figure out how to keep everyone happy—my wife, you in Pennsylvania, Dad in Montana and my in-laws at the other end of the state. Everyone wants something different, but there is only so much to go around."

By this time, I was feeling smaller than an ant—you know, the tiny little red ones. Suddenly the focus had shifted from what I *wanted* to the position in which I had put Josh and Alison. I was the one being selfish, not they. Here he was, making an incredible sacrifice for his country and, at the same time, burdened with how to keep everyone in his family happy. I felt miserable. How had I let this happen? I thought I had learned this lesson already. How had I let my emotions take over—again?

I fought through the tears and forced out the words, "I am so sorry, Josh. I would never refuse to speak to you; you're my son."

When I hung up the phone, the flood came. Ashamed and angry at myself for feeling the way I had, I could hardly believe the way I had spoken to Alison. I had reasoned it all out that I had every right to be angry and hurt, and maybe I did. But I had no right to vent on them. Their burden was much greater than mine. There was only one place I should have been venting, and that was to my heavenly Father. The problem was that I had allowed my human reaction to take control. As I've mentioned in a previous chapter, the key to success is not perfection, which is impossible to achieve. The key is persistence. I needed to get even closer to God. At the first hint of new emotions rolling in, I needed to stop, drop and pray! Another lesson learned the hard way.

Now it's time for the good news. I've mentioned I was on my way to a Women of Faith conference. Once there, I found myself surrounded by thousands of Christian women. How appropriate was that! As usual, God knew when that phone call would take place and had planned the timing perfectly. I spent the next two days drenched in God's grace, mercy and love as it poured over me through songs, praise, worship, and the speakers' messages. I confessed my actions to my heavenly Father, and once again, He set me free. That is the beauty of a relationship with God: we can't use up His forgiveness, His grace, or His mercy. The supply is unlimited and always available when we surrender ourselves to Him. It doesn't matter if we succeed or fail in a particular situation, only that we surrender the outcome to Him. When we succeed, we thank Him for the victory, and when we fail, we seek forgiveness, accept His grace and mercy, and try again. That is all He asks of us.

But God was not the only one of whom I needed to ask forgiveness. A few days later, while chatting on Facebook with Alison, I apologized for my thoughtlessness. I told her I hadn't considered how hard it was on her and Josh to try to divide up the little time off he had among all the family that was tugging at them. "You and Josh need to make your decisions, stick to them, and not worry about what the family thinks," I said, "and I'll work very hard to support your decisions rather than protest them."

Her response amazed me. "I'm just glad we have a strong enough relationship to be able to have open, honest discussions, agree or disagree, and still maintain the bond," she told me. I feel blessed to have such a wonderful daughter-in-law.

This was a huge lesson in handling conflict. Regardless of the situation, we should never react immediately, as that reaction will likely spring from emotions. If we wait, pray, and seek God's counsel, we can respond appropriately and according to His will. Time changes our perspective; we must step back and survey the situation from the other person's point of view. I now ask God to help me see people the way He sees them. Imagine what the world would be like if we all saw each other as God sees us! I cannot yet comprehend how that might look, but I know it would be—literally—heavenly.

CHAPTER 11

Celebrating the Victory

THE FINAL MONTH of Josh's deployment drags on and I wait patiently (or not so much) for his return. I am feeling the effects of this long year. You know how you feel when you have been dealing with something for a long time and you just get tired? That is how I am feeling: worn out and ready for this tour to end.

Our pastor recently presented a series of sermons from the book of Hebrews. One message in particular spoke loudly to me. The first part of this scripture says:

> You have not come to a mountain that can be touched and that is burning with fire; to darkness, gloom and storm; to a trumpet blast or to such a voice speaking words that those who heard it begged that no further word be spoken to them, because they could not bear what was commanded; If even an animal touches the mountain, it must be stoned. The sight was so terrifying that Moses said, 'I am trembling with fear." (Hebrews 12:18-21, *NIV Study Bible*)

Allow me to break this down for you as my pastor did and share how it impacted me. This passage describes a terrible and very frightening mountain, so scary that Moses was trembling. Keep in mind that Moses was the Prince of Egypt. He was a warrior, well trained in combat, yet this mountain caused him to tremble. I feel as if I have visited this mountain over the past few years. There have been times when I have trembled, been overcome with fear, and been filled with uncertainty. I've made mistakes, said and done the wrong things, and hurt others. It's sort of like riding a roller coaster; my emotions have gone up and down based on various situations that occurred during Josh's deployments. The passage goes on to say:

> But you have come to Mount Zion, to the heavenly Jerusalem, the city of the living God. You have come to thousands upon thousands of angels in joyful assembly, to the church of the firstborn, whose names are written in heaven. You have come to God, the judge of all men, to the spirits of righteous men made perfect, to Jesus the mediator of a new covenant, and to the sprinkled blood that speaks a better word than the blood of Abel. (Hebrews 12:22-24, *NIV Study Bible*)

Although the first mountain feels very familiar to me, God tells me I have not come to that mountain, that place of fear. Instead, I have come to Mount Zion, to the very presence of God. I am in assembly with thousands upon thousands of angels and Jesus my Savior. Picture that place for a moment. How can you feel anything but peace in the midst of God's presence, Jesus, and angels?

This really struck me and the lights came on right there in the sanctuary that Sunday morning. I am on the right mountain! Suddenly, I was lifted with a new energy that emanated from the realization of where I was. Even though I've struggled throughout this journey, the paths led me to the right place, exactly where God wanted me to be. I no longer live in fear; I live in the wonderful peace provided by my heavenly Father. This is not something I created, earned, or even deserved but, rather, tranquility extended by the grace of God.

> Rejoice in the Lord always. I will say it again: Rejoice. Let your gentleness be evident to all. The Lord is near. Do not be anxious about anything, but in everything, by prayer and petition, with thanksgiving, present your requests to God. And the peace of God, which transcends all understanding, will guard your hearts and your minds in Christ Jesus.
> (Philippians 4:4-7 *NIV Study Bible*)

I am rejoicing in the Lord and know that He is near. I am praying rather than worrying. And the peace of God truly does transcend all understanding.

The footnote in my study Bible says:

> peace of God: not merely a psychological state of mind, but an
> inner tranquility based on peace with God—the peaceful state of
> those whose sins are forgiven. (Zondervan, *NIV Study Bible*)

My sins are forgiven. I have that inner tranquility, and it is by far the most magnificent feeling one can imagine.

I want you to journey to this place with me for just a moment. Close your eyes and picture yourself sitting on the beach. It's early morning and the sun is just breaking the horizon and casting a beautiful reflection on the water. The waves are calm and the water gently encircles your feet, which are planted in the sand. There is no one else around, just you and the sereneness of the morning. You don't have a care in the world right now. You are not thinking about your job, the kids, or all the things on your to-do list. You are just soaking in the moment.

This is the only way I can describe "inner tranquility" for you. Imagine feeling the way you do at the beach while you're not at the beach. Think about what it would be like to feel that calm in the midst of a regular week at home or even during a crisis. That is the "peace of God".

As I mentioned previously, I attended a Women of Faith conference last month. The theme of the conference was "A Grand New Day", which perfectly describes where I am in my journey. God provides a new beginning each day that I trust everything to Him. This, however, requires me to make a choice. Will I trust Him every day with everything? I can't promise that I will do this without fail, because I am human. Herein lies the beauty of God's grace, I don't have to be perfect.

I am thankful that God brought me to the right mountain and this place of peace. I will rest here and celebrate the victory.

CHAPTER 12

At Last, He Returns!

JOSH RETURNED FROM his second tour in Iraq in mid-August, and I can now write about that deployment, as with the first, in the past tense. His thirty-day block leave was granted from mid-September to mid-October, and he and Alison were scheduled to arrive at our home on October 2nd. My yearlong tour was just about over and I was so excited to see them. When they arrived at Dulles International Airport in Virginia, they called to inform us that their flight from Dulles to State College had been delayed about an hour. It was the last flight out that night and, of course, I started worrying about the possibility that the flight might be cancelled, stranding them at Dulles overnight. My patience was growing thin, and we started making calls to see if they could rent a car to drive the last leg of the trip. We were exploring all options when Josh called back and said the flight was moved back to the original time. What? Was he kidding me? Who ever heard of a delayed flight becoming "undelayed" . . . unbelievable! Josh and Alison arrived on time according to the original itinerary. This was just the first of many blessings during their visit.

They stayed with us for ten days and we had a great time—a big family celebration, complete with reams of photos. It was great to have the whole gang together, which hadn't happened since Josh enlisted in the Army. We also took a short trip to Philadelphia to do some sightseeing. A home Penn State football weekend fell in the middle of Josh and Alison's stay as well. My husband and I have season tickets and always go together. We take our motorhome and tailgate with family and friends. It makes game day twice the fun, and I must admit it is my favorite part.

Josh and Alison were very excited about going to the game, but the early forecast was calling for rain. We decided to wait for game day and make sure the weather was okay, and then we could buy their tickets at the stadium. By Wednesday of that week, the forecast was looking better and the chance of rain was slim. My husband called me from work that day and said he had won two tickets on the fifty-yard line in a contest at work that he didn't even know he was in. If that is not a blessing out of the blue, I don't know what is!

While Josh was home, I was amazed at how much he had matured over the past year. He is a sergeant and has soldiers under his command. His level of responsibility to those men is amazing to me. He said when they go out on missions, one of his guys will always offer to go in front, but he won't let him. He told me, "If someone is going to step on an IED, it will be me. My job is to make sure they get home safely to their families." The selfish side of me was thinking, *You just worry about getting home to your family:* but the mom in me was so proud of his commitment to them, that he was willing to die to protect them. He also talked about the day-to-day stuff. They don't worry every time they go out or even think about getting killed or hurt. They are thinking about how heavy the rucksack on their back is or how hot they are when it is 120 degrees and they are in full gear. They are completely focused on the job they are doing, not worrying about "what if". It is for this purpose that they endure such intense training in boot camp and beyond. It gave me a new perspective on things to know that Josh is not living in fear and worry, but is intent on getting a job done. I learned from my soldier son that I need to focus on the job I am to be doing—which is trusting in God, not worrying about Josh.

What they do worry about is what we are hearing back home. Josh shared that he and his guys were sitting in the mess hall one day when a report came over the news about soldiers getting killed somewhere close by. He immediately thought, *I hope Mom doesn't see this; she'll worry.*

I was pleased to see, when Josh was home, that he had not lost his sense of humor or his need to constantly torment his sisters. The night he arrived, his younger sister, Danielle, did not go to the airport with us because his flight was so late and she had class early the next morning. She knew her brother would get her for this, so she locked her bedroom door. That way, he could not come in and jump on her (as he had done on previous occasions). I protested his expressed intentions of breaking her door down, flattening all of the tires on her car, or siphoning the gas out of its tank; so he decided to put post-it notes all over the windows on her car. This seemed to me the best option, considering the other things he was plotting. She took it well and was quite amused the next morning, as she had to take all the sticky notes off her windows before she could leave for class. This was particularly fun as it had rained overnight and every note was dripping wet. I chuckled as I stood at the window and watched her. I thought she might take all the wet post-its and give them back to her sleeping big brother. But I guess prior experience had taught her that any retaliation from her would escalate what came next from Josh to a whole new level—one she did not care to venture into.

One morning during Josh's visit, Danielle had had enough of her brother's tormenting. After she stomped out of the kitchen, stormed into her bedroom and slammed the door shut, I, for some strange reason, followed her. This was the morning of our big family celebration, so time was in short supply. I thought I could reason with her and go about my day (note to self—you can't reason with 18-year-olds). She was no longer a little girl; she was an adult, sick and tired of everything. After she and I volleyed words back and forth at each other for a bit, Josh entered the room and took command. I stepped back, amazed at how he came in and completely took control of this situation. He lectured his little sister about being disrespectful to her mother and stepfather, and told her that no matter what, you respect your parents. You appreciate all they do for you and the time you have with them. He told her how he regrets the days he spent arguing with me, as he knows now he can never get those days back. He told Danielle he was sorry for tormenting her, that it was all in fun, and he did not realize she was so upset by it. But no matter how she felt about him, he would not tolerate her yelling at her mother. I was in awe at his maturity at 22 years of age. I did have to stop him, though, and tell him gently that Danielle is only 18 and has to figure some of this out in her own time. He cannot expect her to be where he is, as she has not experienced the things that have caused him to mature so quickly. It was a bittersweet conversation, and as proud as I was for his maturity, I was also saddened that his innocence was gone. He seemed to have advanced ten years—time he could never get back. Don't let anyone tell you that soldiers come back the same. They don't, and sometimes they are changed in ways we cannot comprehend. What they see, what they have to do, conditions they have to live in change them, change who they are and how they view things. They have a difficult time readjusting to civilian life and the trivial things that cause us to complain. This is why so many soldiers and families struggle with posttraumatic stress disorder (PTSD). It is so important for families of soldiers to be aware of the signs of PTSD when their soldier returns home. We will talk more about this in the second part of the book.

My son's second deployment has ended, and so has mine. I am more relaxed now that he is in the States and my cell phone is not in my hand 24/7. I have learned many lessons over the past four years. Josh has re-enlisted, so I am certain there will be many more lessons coming. Military life is hard—that is a fact. My son will deploy again, and I know that each deployment will bring new experiences and challenges. But I no longer fear the future or the uncertainties that accompany military life. I can face this life with confidence because I know that God will guide me through any situation.

PART II

Boot Camp for Military Moms

INTRODUCTION

Now that I've told you my story, my successes and failures, it is time to train you to successfully navigate the road ahead. Your experience as the mother of a soldier may be completely different from mine. But, let me equip you with the knowledge that helped *me* to be a survivor—not a victim—of a challenging time.

I must tell you, the information I will provide in the next part of this book is from a Christian perspective. I realize that some of my readers may not share my worldview. I ask you to come along through this part because, Christian or not, we moms of service members need practical ways to endure the multiple deployments that we face. As you read, I hope that each of you will examine the deepest part of your heart and ask the tough questions. Be open and honest when something stirs within you. When you finish the book, keep it handy while you journey through your son's or daughter's deployment. There may come a time when you reach the end of your strength and understanding and realize that you can't make it on your own. My friend, the Lord Jesus Christ will be waiting there for you just as He was for me.

Now, put on your camouflage clothes and your boots; prepare to enter "Boot Camp for Military Moms.

CHAPTER 13

Welcome to Boot Camp

LUCKY FOR YOU, I am not a drill sergeant standing in front of you, my nose an inch from yours, spraying you with saliva as I shout in your face. Don't worry; I am not going to tell you to shave your head, or line up for nine shots and a physical. I won't require a ten-mile run at five in the morning with a forty-pound sack on your back. Our boot camp won't be quite as intense as that which our soldiers have endured. But successful completion will require you to open your heart, be honest with yourself, and be willing to make some changes. Remember, the success our soldiers experienced came from their being broken down, stripped of old habits and then taught the military way. The same is true of us. We must recognize areas that need to be uncovered and retrained.

I have a favorite saying that I like to use with my kids, co-workers, and women in my Bible study class:

Do not be a firefighter—be Smokey Bear!

It is much easier to practice preventive maintenance than to exhaust oneself trying to extinguish a fire. Let's face it: we women are the queens of preventive medicine. We go to what I call our annual "fun visits" to the gynecologist and submit ourselves to Pap smears and mammograms. When our doctor tells us to get a shot or risk coming down with a serious or potentially fatal disease, we get the shot, don't we?

It's one thing to be unaware of a potential danger and end up a victim. It is something different to be aware of a risk and choose to do nothing to defend oneself against it. I have shared the danger with you by telling my story. You know what lies ahead of you. It's now up to you to prepare for it. It's your choice. I pray that you will choose wisely and experience the freedom that I've found.

Now that you know why you're in boot camp, let's get started. The military does a fabulous job of teaching our soldiers everything they need to know in order for them to be prepared for every potential situation. They are taught things we don't even want to think about. Since we are serving alongside them, we also need training so we can become confident in our new role as the mother of a soldier. I will focus on six areas in which our soldiers are trained during boot camp:

DISCIPLINE: The first lesson new soldiers learn the moment they arrive at boot camp is to obey—no matter what. When their foot touches the ground as they step off the bus, they come face to face with their drill sergeant. I am sure you have witnessed this scene in a movie. Drill sergeants scare me! They immediately impart fear and demand surrender. Of course, there are always resistant soldiers who *test the new teacher* and end up facing the ground doing push-ups. Obedience is a matter of life or death for service members; the lives of comrades as well as their own life depends on it. It is irrelevant whether it makes sense or whether they want to—they must obey. When they don't, they suffer harsh consequences, and eventually they learn to obey.

WEAPONS: Soldiers have numerous weapons available to them, and they become proficient with every one. They practice using these weapons continually to develop the skills necessary to make themselves experts. They practice with different weapons, for use in a variety of settings. The battleground is constantly changing, and the weapon of choice must change with it. Action could take place in an urban area, the woods, or a field. Preparedness for all possibilities is critical. The use of weapons becomes second nature to our soldiers; they can react and use them without stopping to think about it.

ARMOR: Soldiers receive various items for protection. One of the first things they receive upon arrival at basic training is immunizations to protect them from diseases. They are issued helmets and bulletproof vests to protect against flying bullets and shrapnel, knee and shoulder pads to protect those areas when they are crawling on the ground, and fireproof gloves in the event they need to reach into a burning vehicle to pull someone out. They are taught which piece goes where, when and how to put it on and when to take it off. Many of the vehicles they ride in are equipped with built-in armor to protect against Improvised Explosive Devices (IEDs) and other explosives.

ENDURANCE: Our soldiers learn how to endure situations that are unimaginable to you and me: living in deplorable conditions, sleeping on the ground or in a vehicle, going days without showers, bearing extreme heat in full gear, and carrying heavy rucksacks and weapons all the time. These are just a few of the conditions that our service members encounter. They are drilled physically to be in the best shape possible and to endure strenuous activity for lengthy periods. Their day does not end at 5:00 PM; they carry on until their mission is complete.

BATTLE READINESS: Soldiers are educated as to who the enemy is, where the threat is and, whenever possible, when the attack will take place. They have practiced endless maneuvers and prepared for every conceivable situation. This training never ends. They train in mock urban communities to become experts on urban warfare. While on deployments, they are briefed prior to every mission as to the specifics of that mission. When a new threat arises, they are taught exactly how to respond to the particulars of it. Training is continuous; as long as they are serving in the military, they will be training.

SURVIVAL: Finally, soldiers learn basic survival skills. In the event that something goes wrong and someone gets hurt, they are taught how to be a first responder, how to save a life, maybe their own. This training seems to be ingrained in our soldiers and becomes part of them even when they are not deployed or even on duty.

Family members need to learn the same kind of lessons that their soldiers experience in basic training. Our training ground is different, and our weapons and armor look nothing like the items our soldiers are given. Our enemy is not the same, and we won't know exactly when our battle will occur. But we do know that enduring our child's deployment will be a challenge and we must be trained for survival.

In the following chapters, we will examine how the lessons our soldiers learn apply to us.

CHAPTER 14

Discipline

THE FIRST LESSON our soldiers learn is discipline—the foundation for all other training. Their first day, they are taught whom to obey. We do not have a commanding officer dictating our daily schedule, telling us when we can eat, speak, sleep, and what we can do in between. If you work outside the home, you have a boss or someone you report to who establishes your priorities for the workday. If you are a stay-at-home mom, your children are likely the ones who determine the day's routine. Other than your boss or the needs of your children, who is in charge or your day? If you are married, your spouse may have some input, but one would hope he is not taking on the role of your commanding officer. You are under your husband's protection and guidance by God's design (Ephesians 5:21-33), but he too must surrender to a higher command.

As adults, who are we to obey? We know we must observe the laws established by various levels of our government, unless we are looking for a not so pleasant vacation behind bars, or a hefty fine. Robbing a bank or hiring a hit man will exact the wrath of the law. We all understand the consequences of neglecting to pay our taxes or speeding in a school zone. We get that stuff. But what about everyday living, as an adult? When we leave our parents' nest, whose counsel guides us?

It may be easier for our soldiers to learn obedience because they start out with a drill sergeant in their face 24/7 telling them exactly what to do, when they have fallen short, and what the consequence will be. When soldiers complete basic training, they are assigned to a squad and usually have a sergeant who continues their training and guidance. They learn that the rules established in the manual are designed to protect them and their fellow soldiers from harm and to teach them to protect one another in battle. When, in some circumstances, they are unable to do that, the one enforcing the rules, their commanding officer, will be the one to put his life on the line to save them.

Do you ever think, as I do, *I wish I were a kid again and had mom telling me what to do, where to go (or not), and setting curfews?* I hope, as adults, we have all come to appreciate that our "mean", "horrible", parents, who were always telling us what to do and making our lives "miserable", were also guiding and protecting us. Though we didn't comprehend it then, there was a sense of security in knowing that someone else was in charge and would rescue us if we got in trouble.

Who provides guidance and security for us now—as adults? Who sets the rules and consequences that will keep us safe? Who rescues us when we cannot rescue ourselves?

If you are a Christian, as I am, your Commander-in-Chief is God the Father. We are to obey Him. But how does one obey God? What does that even mean on a daily basis?

The good news is, God provided us with a "manual", the Bible, and He makes it clear that any failure to obey His instructions, whether great or small, puts us in mortal danger. And because we are humans, incapable of perfection (Isaiah 53:6a), we are all lawbreakers (Romans 3:23, James 2:10). We have inherited the tendency to break the law from the very first humans, Adam and Eve, who took advantage of the free will God gave them and used that freedom to disobey Him (Genesis 3). The consequence for all of us who disobey God is death—spiritual death (Romans 6:23); but our Commander-in-Chief has come to our rescue. He has dispatched none other than His Son—God's perfectly obedient General, if you will—not only to explain the battle plan to us, but to take upon Himself the consequences of our blunders. Jesus came, literally, to save your life and mine by voluntarily dying on a Roman cross—the perfectly obedient One for the less-than-perfect ones—so that we could survive the war. He has defeated our enemy, Satan, whose object was to destroy us. He has defeated sin and death, once and for all, so that we can be discharged with honor and proceed to our beautiful eternal Home when our life here on earth ends. What freedom, joy, and peace the grace of God through Jesus Christ, His Son, has provided for us!

But while we are still serving here on this battlefield called Earth, Jesus our General has a word or two for us concerning obedience. Just before His battle with death, He told His followers, "Do not let your hearts be troubled. Trust in God; trust also in me" (John 14:1, *NIV*

Study Bible)). Following Jesus' crucifixion and after He had risen from the dead and appeared to ten of His disciples, Thomas, the one who had been absent when all of these things occurred, told the others he would not believe that Jesus had been resurrected unless he could put his finger into the nail wounds and his hand into Jesus' pierced side. Then, Jesus appeared to him, offered him that opportunity, and said, "Stop doubting and believe" (John 20:27, *NIV Study Bible*). "My Lord and my God," Thomas replied (verse 28).

We might say that the above commands are two of the most important that Jesus provided to us: to trust in God and in Him, and to stop doubting and believe. Your victory—and mine—is won. We have conquered death, both physical and spiritual, through Jesus. Obedience now consists of having faith in Him and His finished work of rescue. We serve under Him now simply to enhance His glory. We reach out in love to others in order to expand His joyful army and further His kingdom. In the Great Commission, Jesus tells us, "Therefore go and make disciples of all nations, baptizing them in the name of the Father and of the Son and of the Holy Spirit, and teaching them to **obey everything I have commanded you.**" (Matthew 28:19-20 *NIV Study Bible*, emphasis mine). His primary instructions, as we've stated, are to stop doubting, to believe, and to trust in the Father and the Son. This brings peace, the beginning of joy. And speaking of joy . . . In Luke 11, while Jesus was teaching His listeners about evil spirits, a woman called out (verses 27, 28), "Blessed is the mother who gave you birth and nursed you." Jesus replied, "Blessed rather are those who **hear the word of God and obey it.**" (Luke 11:27-28, *NIV Study Bible*, emphasis mine). What a powerful statement! "Blessed" means "happy". Jesus is not denying the blessedness of Mary in bearing and nursing Him as a baby and watching Him grow into a wonderful teacher; He is stressing that we will be *even happier than this* if we follow Him. Jesus came to fulfill all the law (because we could not) and the prophets (because He is the promised Messiah). By the grace of God, He now lives in each person who accepts Him as Lord and Savior (Revelation 3:20), so that we no longer have to be perfect to gain entrance to God's heavenly kingdom and live eternally. Jesus has gladly given us His perfection as a free gift from our heavenly Commander (Hebrews 2:9).

We've covered *who and what* we must obey, and the above passage in Luke tells us *why* we should obey—because He commands it and we will be blessed. Do you remember, as a kid, asking your mom, "Why do I have to do that?" She would answer, "Because I said so." When we obeyed mom things went well, and when we didn't obey her we would end up in trouble. As adults, we can appreciate that her rules were for our own protection, because she loved us. The same is true of our heavenly Father. If you can imagine how much your mom loves you, multiply that to the nth power to get some idea of how much God loves you. In fact, God's love for us is so great that He gave His only Son that we would have eternal life—with Him (John 3:16). We cannot obey God enough to earn our way into heaven; the only way to get to heaven is to accept Jesus Christ as our personal Lord and Savior and receive perfection through Him. Once we do that, we have peace in God's promise of eternity. Our loving heavenly Father has a generous supply of grace to cover us when we fail in our attempts to be obedient *if* we offer sincere confession and repentance; we know He will forgive us (1 John 1:9).

While our obedience may not be a matter of physical life or death, as it is for our soldiers, it does play a critical role in determining the quality of our earthly life. Likewise, God's grace is plentiful, but it does not eliminate the consequences of our sin here on earth. I must confess that my biggest failures in life have come at times when I was not being obedient to Jesus' commands but was doing things my way. I want to tell you, from my personal experience, His way is always, one-hundred percent of the time, better than our way.

You may be asking, how do I start obeying Jesus' commands? In the verse above from Luke, Jesus says, " . . . hear the Word of God and obey it." To hear the word of God, you must get into the Word. Spend time reading your Bible. The Ten Commandments (Exodus 20:1-17) provide the foundation for all moral behavior. We should try our best to follow them. The Gospels (Matthew, Mark, Luke, and John) give us a fine account of Jesus' life and teachings, as well as His death and resurrection. In John 13:34 He commands us to love one another as He has loved us, and in Luke 6:31 He instructs us to treat others as we would have them treat us—"the Golden Rule". The book of Romans explains the plan of salvation and how it was accomplished. Study the Word and then pray. Ask God to give you the will to obey and to live for Him even when you don't want to—and, believe me, there will be those times.

Once you put aside your will and obey God's instead, you'll begin to see your heart, hardened and calloused by life, change to a heart of gratitude and obedience to Him. In time, because of your new desire to follow Him, God will help you break your old desires, allowing His will to flourish in you. Have you heard the saying "Die to self daily"? That is exactly what you have to do: lay down your will every day and let God's will lead you. Invite the Holy Spirit to help you. As I've said, I have tried it both ways, God's and mine, and repeatedly my will has led me to places I should not have been. Look at it this way: our will is formed by our limited view of a situation; God's will is couched in His omniscient view of everything. He knows which roads lead to disasters and which lead to blessings.

I think back to Josh's first deployment, when I did not want to lead the Bible study I was offered but trusted God had placed the opportunity before me. I had no idea, at that time, why I was to lead that study. I look back now and see clearly that God wanted me to go where He led me so that He could provide exactly what I needed to get through that very difficult time. Suppose I hadn't been obedient to His leading; how would I have survived that time?

I challenge you to think of yourself as a Bradley fighting vehicle (Infantry fighting vehicle) heading to war. Who do you want sitting in the driver's seat? I drove myself into battle many times and ended up off the side of the road, in a ditch; I have battle scars to prove it. God is now in my driver's seat. That does not mean my life is perfect; it is not. It means that when a situation comes up that is troubling, I stop and ask myself a question or two: What would Jesus do in my place? How does the Bible instruct me to respond to this kind of problem? I pray for His wisdom and guidance to do the right thing. *Ask* God. I often ask Him to make things obvious to me, to open or close a door. You are not going to surprise God by telling Him you are confused. He already knows that. Asking God for guidance is showing Him that you are placing your trust in Him. He will answer you.

Often God gives you the answer through another person. I have sought counsel from godly women many times and have asked those in my Bible study group to pray for me when I needed direction. I treasure the intimate fellowship that I have with these women. We laugh and cry together. Sometimes we have to say difficult things to one another, but we do it in a spirit of love because that is what God calls us to do. I cannot overstress the need we have to surround ourselves with godly women and to study God's Word together.

I hope you realize the importance of trusting and obeying God out of a sense of gratitude for His grace, extended to you through His Son. Once you have accepted Jesus Christ as your personal Lord and Savior, obedience is the next step in experiencing the fullness of life. I pray you will examine your heart and be open to change as you surrender your driver's seat to your Heavenly Father.

I want to bind this difficult lesson on obedience with a story that reveals a beautiful picture of grace that I heard years ago at a women's retreat.

A potter was setting up a display of his work; each pot was unique and crafted by his hands. A few were perfect; not one scratch, no holes or uneven spots. Most had cracks, holes, rough spots, and other imperfections. People were gathering around the table and marveling over the flawless pieces. The potter noticed all the attention was on the perfect ones and said, "They are not finished yet." The crowd stepped back as he began to place lit candles in each of the pots. Each piece took on a new appearance. The flawless ones were lovely with the light shining through the opening on the top. The imperfect ones were stunningly exquisite, each one in its own way. It was the cracks and the holes that allowed the light from within to shine through to create a magnificent piece of hand-made art.

My friends, we are the clay pots and God is the potter. All the cracks, scratches, rough spots, and holes that some might consider imperfections are evidence of our loving Father's forgiveness (through Jesus Christ), grace, and healing. The apostle Paul tells us, "And we know that in all things God works for the good of those who love him, who have been called according to his purpose (Romans 8:28, *NIV Study Bible*). This scripture does not say in "some things" or "good things"; it says "in all things". That means our blotches and failures too. The prophet Isaiah says, "Yet, O Lord, you are our Father. We are the clay, you are the potter; we are all the work of your hand" (Isaiah 64:8, *NIV Study Bible*).

When you accept the precious grace of God, He will use the brokenness of your life to extend His light to others by transforming you into a shining example of God's love and grace.

Summary

- God is your Commander-in-Chief and you must trust and obey Him, because He loves you and wants to protect you.

- Spend time in the Word. Start by reading the Gospels to learn what Jesus commands and what He provides for us.

- When you start going against your desires and obeying God's commands instead, you'll begin to notice your will decreasing and God's will increasing in your daily life.

- When you fail—and you will fail—don't beat yourself up. Ask forgiveness, accept God's grace, and in persistence move forward, following Him. Remember, your perfection comes through Christ.

- Remember, too, that you are a picture of God's grace, and every sin you have confessed to Him has been transformed to make of you a beautiful vessel for His magnificent light to shine through.

- If you do not know Jesus Christ as your personal Lord and Savior, please consider praying the prayer below now and come under God's protection.

Heavenly Father,

I want to have the assurance of spending eternity in Heaven with You. I believe that you sent your son, Jesus Christ, to die on the cross for my sin. I now confess my sins before You, repent of them, and ask Jesus Christ to come into my heart. I desire to have a personal relationship with Him and live each day in gratitude for your forgiveness, provided through Him.

Thank you, Lord! Amen.

If you prayed this prayer—please tell someone today! I am thrilled that you are now part of the family of God. I want you to make the most of your new relationship with Jesus Christ, and to do that you really need to have a Christian friend to guide your growth. Congratulations on making the best decision of your life!

Now, begin each day of your new spiritual journey with prayer seeking wisdom for the day. Here is an example of how you might pray.

Father God,

I praise You for Who You are. I honor You for all that You have done and continue to do for me through the gift of your Son, Jesus. Lord, Your Word tells me to be obedient to Your will, not mine. I ask You, God, to search my heart today for areas in which I'm clinging to my will instead of submitting to Your will. Lord, I ask that You reveal these areas to me, that I might confess them to You, and I ask that You give me the wisdom and strength to surrender these areas to Your will.

Father, I trust You completely and ask You to lead me to the place where You want me to be. Give me the will to obey You in all things today.

I ask this in Jesus' name. Amen.

CHAPTER 15

Battle Readiness

LET'S SKIP ahead to the battle readiness part of our training, because it is important to know what our battle looks like before we try to prepare for it.

Once our soldiers complete basic training and are assigned to their duty station, they immediately begin training for deployment to a specific place. Prior to Josh's going to Iraq, both times, he trained specifically for Iraq. Now that he is home, his unit is currently training for their next deployment, to Afghanistan. Training must be different as the terrain there is very rugged and mountainous. The equipment and weapons employed will change, to adapt to new territory. Therefore, it is vital to the soldiers' success to train according to the specific conditions they will encounter while deployed.

As mothers of service members, we must understand the battle we are heading into so we can be adequately prepared. Unlike our sons and daughters, we don't have to fly to the other side of the world to find our battle. Most often, we don't find our battle at all—it finds us.

Rather than a physical battle against human beings, our battle begins in our mind. The Bible describes this battle and the equipment we need for it in Ephesians 6:

> Finally, be strong in the Lord and in his mighty power. Put on the full armor of God so that you can take your stand against the devil's schemes. For our struggle is not against flesh and blood, but against the rulers, against the authorities, against the powers of this dark world and against the spiritual forces of evil in the heavenly realms. Therefore, put on the full armor of God, so that when the day of evil comes, you may be able

---

to stand your ground, and after you have done everything, to stand (Ephesians 6:10-13, *NIV Study Bible*).

Now you may be thinking, *What have I ever done to the devil that would make him want to wage war against me?* If you have not yet accepted Jesus Christ as your personal Lord and Savior, Satan wants to keep you from making that decision. If you have accepted Christ, Satan knows that he has lost you to God's kingdom. He can and will do everything in his power to keep you from winning others to Christ. His new goal is to make you as ineffective as possible so you will not be working for God. He wants to tear you down and make you feel defeated and discouraged. He does this by telling you lies about yourself, your family, your marriage, your job, or any situation where you are vulnerable.

When your child enlisted in the military, you became susceptible to new emotions such as fear and uncertainty. Satan may use these against you the same way he used them against me. Think back to my personal story that took place when Josh was serving his first tour in Iraq. I was in fear constantly for his safety. In that condition, I was not displaying God's grace, love, and mercy; in fact, the only thing I was exhibiting was Satan's power and how I had allowed it to control me. Why would a non-Christian watching me, a proclaimed Christian in that condition, want to make a decision for Christ? Would someone *want* a life of fear and torment? Absolutely not! I was right where Satan wanted me, completely focused on my fear, submissive to his power, and not being a good witness for Christ. Fortunately, I was part of a women's Bible study group and had support from Christian women. I knew I couldn't help myself, so I prayed and asked others to pray for me. God answered those prayers and provided me with the truth and knowledge I needed to protect myself.

It is imperative that you, as the mother of a service member, have a support system. Surround yourself with other military moms who are experiencing the same challenges you are. You can guide one another when things get rough by sharing experiences and lessons learned.

I would like to emphasize one other point about the passage in Ephesians. In verse 13, Paul does not say "*if* the day of evil comes", he says "*when* the day of evil comes". It is not a matter of *if;* it is a matter of *when.* The apostle Peter tells us, "Be self-controlled and alert. Your enemy the devil prowls around like a roaring lion looking for someone to devour" (1 Peter 5:8, *NIV Study Bible*).

In addition to being a military mom, you may be at risk of Satan's attacks if you are clinging to unresolved issues. In his second letter to the church at Corinth, Paul says this: "The reason I wrote you was to see if you would stand the test and be obedient in everything. If you forgive anyone, I also forgive him. And what I have forgiven—if there was anything to forgive—I have forgiven in the sight of Christ for your sake, in order that Satan might not outwit us. For we are not unaware of his schemes" (2 Corinthians 2:9-11). Paul is telling us not to withhold forgiveness from anyone so that we do not give Satan the upper hand. In chapter 11 he says, "For such men are false apostles, deceitful workmen, masquerading as apostles of Christ. And no wonder, for Satan himself masquerades as an angel of light. It is not surprising, then, if his servants masquerade as servants of righteousness. Their end will be what their actions deserve (2 Corinthians 11:13-15 *NIV Study Bible*).

One thing you must understand about Satan is that he is not going to tempt you with ugly, smelly, unpleasant, repulsive ideas. He is going to taunt you with delicious, lovely, appealing things that are hard to resist. He will try to get you to buy into something that is easy to fall for, easy to believe. Look what he did to Adam and Eve in the garden; he didn't tempt Eve with a shriveled up dry old prune. He teased her with a beautiful piece of fruit; Genesis describes the fruit of the tree as "good for food and pleasing to the eye" (Genesis 3:6). Satan is the master of lies; he knows what your weaknesses are and he will use them to trick you.

What can you do to protect yourself from Satan and his schemes? James tells us, "Submit yourselves, then, to God. Resist the devil, and he will flee from you" (James 4:14, *NIV Study Bible*). Do you remember the first part of the scripture we looked at earlier from Ephesians? "Finally, be strong in the Lord and in his mighty power. Put on the full armor of God so that you can take your stand against the devil's schemes (Ephesians 6:10, 11, *NIV Study Bible*).

So get ready to explore the protective covering that God has provided for us. If you have not yet accepted Jesus Christ as your Savior, please give serious thought to making that decision and coming under the protection of God's armor. For those of you who know Jesus as your Lord and Savior, it is time to get suited up.

Summary

- Remember your battle is spiritual rather than physical. It begins in your mind, and you must be prepared for it.

- Surround yourself with a network of support—Christian women and other military moms.

- Identify areas of vulnerability where you need to be extra cautious.

- Satan is the master of lies and he will try to deceive you. Don't give in. If you have accepted Jesus Christ as your Savior, you have power over Satan.

Prayer:

Father God,

Thank you for providing me with protection against Satan's schemes. I ask You to open my mind as I explore the armor that will enable me to resist him. I ask You to guard my mind and my heart from attacks. Father, help me to develop a network of support to surround me during the difficult times.

I ask this in Jesus name. Amen.

CHAPTER 16

Armor

I am doing a quick mental scan of my home and I am quite certain I do not have anything here that would qualify as a weapon or armor. I guess the Cutco knives in my kitchen could be weapons, or perhaps the golf clubs in the garage would work if I needed to chase someone away. The only armor I can come up with is my winter coat to protect against the cold Colorado winds, which I've been told are brutal. As of this writing, my husband and I have just moved to this state and I have not yet experienced a winter here.

The weapons and armor we will explore look very different from those of our service members. They get knives, pistols, hand grenades, just to mention a few of those they carry on their person. Army infantrymen have much larger weapons at their disposal when they are out in the field inside their Bradley fighting machines. Service members in all branches have a variety of weapons available to them because there are different risks. They are trained to know which weapon to use and when. It is important to match up the weapon with the risk in order to win the battle.

I love the Old Testament story of David and Goliath. David was very successful going into battle against Goliath with just a sling and five tiny stones. I am relieved that our soldiers have much larger and more powerful weapons at their disposal. Yet, we know that David had God on his side in that battle, and that is what makes any weapon sufficient.

Ephesians 6:14-18 lists the weapons and armor that God provides for us. Let's look at them individually so we can see how they apply specifically to us as mothers of service members.

In this chapter, we will focus on the ones that work as armor, things we must put on:

BELT OF TRUTH

In the first part of verse 14, Paul says, "Stand firm then, with the belt of truth buckled around your waist" (Ephesians 6:14, *NIV Study Bible*). What is truth, and where does it come from?

In John 18, Jesus says, " . . . for this reason I was born, and for this I came into the world, to testify to the truth . . ." (John 18: 37, *NIV Study Bible*).

If you are a child of God, your truth is in God's Word. Spending time in the Word is your first line of defense. Everything else depends upon the truth.

For Roman soldiers, the belt was the centerpiece of all their armor; everything else connected to the belt. If the belt was in the wrong place or not properly fastened, the other armor might not be effective in protecting them. The same is true for us. If we have not found the source of truth, we are in danger of being unprotected.

What are some truths about our role as a parent of a soldier? Here are a few that I have learned:

- We are not in control, but God is.
- We will miss our child terribly, but God can give us peace.
- We will not know where our child is all the time, but God will.
- Our child will be in danger, but God can protect him or her.
- Our worrying cannot change the outcome of any situation, but prayer can.
- Satan wants us to worry, but we have power over Satan.

If we understand the entire truth about a situation we are facing, we can respond with the knowledge of that truth. The unknown is usually what makes us fall. Think about it: when was the last time you tripped on something? Maybe a stick or stone was in your path, a hole in the sidewalk or a turned-up corner of the rug. You tripped because you did not know that something was there—you were not looking for it. If there had been a sign that said, "Beware—Danger Ahead", you would have been looking out for it and would likely have avoided tripping.

When Josh first enlisted in the Army, I had no idea what the road ahead of me looked like. No one told me there was danger that I needed to prepare for. I entered that situation with no knowledge of the truth. I was completely blind to the fact that I was heading into battle; therefore, as I pressed ahead, I ended up right in the middle of it. Once I became aware of the challenges I faced as the mother of a soldier, I was able to prepare myself to be successful. You must do the same. No excuses; now you know. Buckle your belt of truth.

BREASTPLATE OF RIGHTEOUSNESS

The second part of verse 14 says, "with the breastplate of righteousness in place" (Ephesians 6:14, *NIV Study Bible*).

When I think of a breastplate, I think of the movie *Troy*. When Achilles prepared to go to battle, he put on a breastplate. That piece of armor protected the core of the body, where all the vital organs are located. Our service members wear bulletproof vests that protect their core, as well.

Our core protection as noted in this scripture is the breastplate of righteousness. Let's look at the definition of righteousness to gain a better understanding.

Webster defines righteous like this: *1. acting in a just, upright manner; virtuous: as, a righteous man. 2. morally right or justifiable: as, a righteous act.*

Our character shapes this piece of protective armor. If you are a Christian, your character should be defined by your identity in Christ. I say *should* because many Christians do not know or understand their identity in Christ. I was one of them when Josh first enlisted in the Army. I knew I had accepted Jesus as my Savior when I turned 12 and was baptized. I knew that if I died I would go to Heaven and spend eternity there. But I never fully understood what my eternal salvation provided for me here on earth. When you accept Jesus Christ as your Lord and Savior, you are given a helper to guide you through life.

Jesus promises this helper to His disciples in John 14:

> "I will ask the Father and He will give you another Counselor to be with you forever, the Spirit of truth. The world cannot accept him, because it neither sees him nor knows him. But

you know him, for he lives with you and will be in you." (John 14:16-18, *NIV Study Bible*)

Then in verse 26, Jesus goes on to say,

> "The counselor, the Holy Spirit, whom the Father will send in my name, will teach you all things and will remind you of everything I have said to you." (John 14:26, *NIV Study Bible*)

When you acknowledge the Holy Spirit within you by living in faith, the Spirit produces fruit. Paul writes in Galatians 5:

> . . . but the fruit of the Spirit is love, joy, peace, patience, kindness, goodness, faithfulness, gentleness and self-control. Against such things there is no law. Those who belong to Christ Jesus have crucified the sinful nature with its passions and desires. Since we live by the Spirit, let us keep in step with the Spirit. (Galatians 5:22-25, *NIV Study Bible*) The footnote in my *NIV study Bible* explains it like this:
> "Christian character is produced by the Holy Spirit, not by mere moral discipline of trying to live by the law" (Zondervan, *NIV Study Bible*).

Do you get what this means? We don't have to attain perfection; we just have to acknowledge, by faith, that the Holy Spirit lives in us and allow the Spirit to guide us. This is wonderful, as it does not require us to be super spectacular people. It does, however, encourage us to be faithful to God and His will for us.

Achilles had a choice: he could put on his breastplate and be protected or choose not to put it on and expose himself to danger. His risk of death greatly increased if he chose not to put it on.

The same is true of us. If we choose to acknowledge the Holy Spirit living in us and understand the power that comes with that, we are wearing our breastplate of righteousness, knowing that the protection lies within us, in the Holy Spirit. This is very important to us as mothers of service members. Understanding the power we're given by the Holy Spirit enables us to have control over situations that we are faced with rather than allowing those situations to control us. I learned how this works during Josh's first deployment, while I was leading the Neil Anderson study, *Breaking Through to Spiritual Maturity*. It opened my eyes to my identity in Christ and the power that comes with it. Once you know this and apply these truths to your life, you can stand firm in your faith throughout every storm that comes your way, knowing that the Holy Spirit is guiding you.

Military mom, put that breastplate on.

FEET FITTED WITH READINESS

Paul describes our next piece of armor in verse 15: "and with feet fitted with the readiness that comes from the gospel of peace" (Ephesians 6:15, *NIV Study Bible*).

Now, you are probably getting excited at the thought of feet, because that means we will be talking about shoes, and what woman does not want to talk about shoes? How many pairs of shoes do you own? According to several different surveys I found online, the average woman owns 19 pairs of shoes. We have shoes for every occasion, don't we? We have shoes for work, play, exercise, hiking, shopping, dancing, church, formal wear, and I am sure there are others I have not mentioned. In addition to shoes for every situation, we must have shoes that go with certain outfits. High-heeled boots are great with skirts or jeans, but you wouldn't wear them with a dress. Women need options!

There is one necessary pair of shoes that you may not have, and if you do have them, they are not sitting on the shoe rack in your closet.

The verse we are looking at says, *"have your feet fitted with readiness"*. How do you do that? Does readiness come in all sizes? If we read on, it states, *"readiness that comes from the gospel of peace"*. Where do we get peace? If you recall the passage from Galatians 5:22, one of the fruits of the Spirit is peace. When we accept Jesus Christ as our Savior and acknowledge the Holy Spirit in us, peace is part of the package. Now, you may be thinking you know many Christians who do not seem to have a lot of peace. This is very true and was true of me as well. Peace, just like other fruits of the Spirit, has to be put into practice. When you buy new shoes, you don't just take them home and shove the box to the back of the closet, do you? Of course not; you wear them. They may be uncomfortable at first, but in time, they fit perfectly.

The problem with many Christians is they accept Jesus Christ as their Savior and then take Him home and put Him on a shelf, as if they are saving Him for a rainy day. My friend, please do not wait for the storm to come; you must prepare for it ahead of time. Look back to the scripture from verse 25 of Galatians: *"Since we live by the Spirit, let us keep in step with the Spirit."* That means we are required to take action. It does not say, "since we live by the Spirit, let us put Him on a shelf and do nothing."

How does one produce peace? As you trust God in situations and He gets you through, your faith grows, and soon you will discover that your trust is so strong that no matter what storm shows up, you can find peace. I love this passage from Philippians 4:

> Do not be anxious about anything, but in everything, by prayer and petition, with thanksgiving, present your requests to God. And the peace of God, which transcends all understanding, will guard your hearts and your minds in Christ Jesus. (Philippians 4:6-7, *NIV Study Bible*)

Do we as mothers of service members have anything to be anxious about? Absolutely, but our being anxious is not going to accomplish anything. Pray, pray, pray, and then pray some more.

During both of Josh's deployments in Iraq, I would pray every night when I went to bed. There was an eight-hour time difference, so when I was going to bed, he was just starting his day. I would pray for his protection for that day, no matter where he was or what he was doing. I prayed for protection for his entire unit. During the two 12-month tours in Iraq, not one person in Josh's immediate unit was seriously injured. Praise God!

Unless you have experienced the peace of God, which transcends all understanding, you cannot fathom how one can find peace in the midst of a fearful situation. I have experienced it, and it truly surpassed my comprehension. God is guarding your heart and mind in the midst of a storm. Do you know anyone else who can do that?

If you know Jesus Christ as your Lord and Savior, He has a new pair of shoes waiting for you. They are the best fitting pair of shoes you will ever wear. The good news is they go with every outfit in your closet and they work for every occasion. My pastor called them your "Be still and know that I am God" shoes. Put them on every morning. You fit these shoes to your feet by applying God's Word to your life.

Would you want your child heading into battle without his or her combat boots? No. So why would you? Go get those shoes on!

HELMET OF SALVATION

The next piece of armor is by far the most important: "Take the helmet of salvation" (Ephesians 6:17, *NIV Study Bible*).

The helmet is the most important piece of armor for our service members, as it protects their heads.

Think back to the last football game you attended. When the quarterback ran onto the field, did he have something on his head? Of course he did; he wore a helmet. Now imagine your reaction if he had not worn a helmet. You probably would have stood up and shouted out, "Hey, you forgot something!" Just as our soldiers and football players need helmets to protect the head, we need a helmet also.

The helmet described in the verse above refers to our salvation. It is our guarantee that we will spend eternity in Heaven with our Lord and Savior.

Let's look at a conversation between Jesus and His disciples in the Gospel of John. Jesus is encouraging them:

> "Do not let your hearts be troubled. Trust in God; trust
> also in me. In my Father's house are many rooms: if it were
> not so, I would have told you. I am going there to prepare
> a place for you. And if I go and prepare a place for you, I
> will come back and take you to be with me that you also
> may be where I am. You know the way to the place where
> I am going."
> Thomas said to Jesus, "Lord, we don't know where you
> are going, so how can we know the way?"

> Jesus answered him, "I am the way and the truth and the life. No one comes to the Father except through me."(John 14:1-6 *NIV, Study Bible*)

Do you want to have a room in the Father's house? I do! I have peace in knowing that I have a room because I have accepted Jesus Christ as my personal Savior. This passage tells us that the only way to guarantee you will have a room in Heaven is by accepting Jesus' substitutionary death on the cross as payment for your sins.

I hope that you have received Jesus Christ as your personal Savior, even if you just did it as you read the previous chapter. Salvation is the foundation of our personal relationship with Jesus Christ. That relationship is what carried me through my son's deployments.

If you have not yet made this decision, it is my prayer that you will in the near future. I encourage you to read, explore and do whatever research you need to do to answer any questions that may be preventing you from making this decision.

Now, I want you to go find a mirror and imagine yourself wearing the armor we've covered. Do you like what you see? You are now dressed head to toe with protection from God. It is up to you to put these things on, every day when you get up. You have the knowledge; the question is—will you use it?

Summary

- Get dressed for victory every morning, no exceptions.

- Put on your helmet of salvation first and come under God's protection.

- Buckle the belt of truth around your waist. Stick with the facts—what you know to be true. Don't spend time on "what ifs".

- Protect your core with the breastplate of righteousness. Know your identity in Christ and understand the power that comes with being a child of God through Him.

- Get your shoes on. Be ready for anything that comes your way by having the peace of God as your foundation.

Prayer:

Heavenly Father,

I ask You to reveal these truths clearly to me. Father, I want to experience freedom in knowing who I am in Christ; help me to achieve this. Help me daily to wear the salvation, truth, righteousness and peace that You provide for my protection. Stand by me through every challenge that comes my way.

Thank You for being my faithful Commander. Amen.

CHAPTER 17

Weapons

NOW THAT WE are suited up, head to toe, with protection, we need to explore the weapons we will use to defend ourselves in battle. Similar to the armor you are sporting, the weapons are not physical—they are spiritual, for ours is a spiritual battle. There are two weapons, and we find them both in Ephesians 6. We will cover the sword of the Spirit in this chapter and the shield of faith in the next chapter.

SWORD OF THE SPIRIT

The second part of verse 17 says, "and the sword of the Spirit, which is the word of God" (Ephesians 6:17, *NIV Study Bible*).

Swords are not the weapon of choice anymore for our military. This is a good thing because using a sword requires one to be very close to the enemy. If you have watched any movies about wars of long ago, you noticed that the combatants charged into one another. I never understood how, with so many soldiers that close together, they could know who they were striking with their swords.

I am thankful that our soldiers have better weapons at their disposal, such as rifles, grenades, mortars, and other long range artillery that don't require hand to hand combat. Now, imagine our soldiers setting out on their mission without any of these weapons. How could they possibly hope to be successful or even survive?

It is the same for us. As mothers of service members, we need weapons too. One weapon is the sword referenced in the passage above: the Word of God. In the Gospel of John, we find this explanation:

"In the beginning was the Word, and the Word was with God, and the Word was God." . . . "The Word became flesh, and made his dwelling among us." (John 1:1, 14a *NIV Study Bible*)

This refers to Jesus' coming to earth to live among us. God's Word is God speaking to us through those He called to write down the words He revealed to them, both foretelling and detailing Jesus' life, death, and resurrection. If God were standing in front of you right now speaking to you, would you be reading the words on this page or paying attention to what God was saying to you? Can you fathom what it would be like to have God speaking directly to you? Well, don't imagine anymore. Go get your Bible, because God is speaking directly to you from its pages.

Just as our soldiers learn the use of any weapon, we must learn how to use our Bible. The only way to do that is to get into your Bible consistently. Our soldiers learn very early in basic training how to use their weapon, how to fire it, how to take it apart and clean it, and how to fix it if something happens to it. They spend countless hours at the firing range practicing the use of their weapon and gaining skill in hitting their target.

We must do the same; we need to spend countless hours in God's Word, learning how to live and how not to live. The Word of God is what feeds us spiritually and helps us to grow into mature, battle-ready Christians. As we read the Bible, we gain knowledge and understanding that develops our faith and helps to keep our path straight.

You may be thinking, *I try to read the Bible, but it's confusing and I don't understand what it means.* This frustration is very common, and I struggled with it for many years. I strongly urge you to get involved in a Bible study group. This is a great way to break down specific passages and make sense of them, adding daily to your overall comprehension. Keep in mind that God reveals His word to us in different ways. I have been in Bible study groups where the members would read a scripture and each would find a different meaning in those same words. God will open our eyes and hearts to particular scriptures and applications at different times. If you think about it, we are all at different places in our spiritual journey. Someone who is new to this journey may not get the same thing out of a scripture verse as someone who is very mature spiritually. As we grow in our spiritual maturity, we will gain new understanding from scripture. The more you grow, the more you will want to reach the next level.

It is very important to pray before you read your Bible. Ask God to open your eyes to what you are about to read and to reveal its truth. I often ask God to remove all distractions from my head before I read my Bible, because my mind becomes occupied with life issues and leaves little room for more information to get in. Remember, you are not going to shock God by asking Him to clear your thoughts. He already knows the condition of your mind and it will please Him if you ask for the clutter to be removed to make room for what He wants to give you.

Find a quiet place daily, get your Bible and spend time with God.

Summary

- Our best weapon is our Bible, start reading it today.

- Set aside a certain time each day when you can go to a quiet place and read your Bible. Start with just ten minutes a day; as you grow you will want more.

- When you read your Bible, God is speaking directly to you.

- Join a Bible study group where you can examine portions of the Word of God with others.

- Ask God to open your eyes and heart to see and accept His Word.

Prayer:

Heavenly Father,

Thank You for Your Word. Thank You for loving me so much that You gave me Your Word as a means to communicate Your truths to me. I ask You, Lord, to open my eyes to see, my ears to hear and my heart to receive Your Word and be able to apply it to my life.

Father, I ask You to reveal to me the truths that I need in order to continue my spiritual growth. I ask You to direct me to a group of Christian women with whom I can fellowship and study Your Word.

Thank You, Lord, for who You are and all that You do for me. Amen.

CHAPTER 18

Endurance

OUR SERVICE MEMBERS start physical training almost immediately upon arrival at boot camp. They are up before the sun; go out on many-mile road marches and long runs, do countless push-ups and sit-ups, and perform many other challenging exercises. The military focuses a great deal on getting their soldiers as physically strong as they can be. Service members are required to pass periodic tests to ensure they are physically fit for battle. This physical strength is what enables them to endure the extreme conditions they face on deployments.

We, too, must be strong so we can endure our child's deployments. While physical strength may not be the most important type of strength we need, it is important. I do encourage you to get into a regular exercise program. Physical strength contributes a great deal to our mental and spiritual strength.

SHIELD OF FAITH

The final protection we will look at serves as both a weapon and armor. It is what I believe enables us to endure whatever comes our way. "In addition to all this, take up the shield of faith, with which you can extinguish all the flaming arrows of the evil one." (Ephesians 6:16, *NIV Study Bible*)

The first part of this verse, *"In addition to all this"*, refers to the armor that we discussed in the previous chapter. Now that you have this armor on, it is time to "take up the shield of faith". What is the shield of faith? My study Bible compares it to: "the large Roman shield covered with leather, which could be soaked in water and used to put out flame-tipped arrows". (Zondervan, *NIV Study Bible*)

This shield protects you once you have taken hold of it, and you can use it to fend off any attack from the enemy.

We have already determined that our enemy is Satan and his goal is to attack us with lies to keep us from growing in faith and advancing the Kingdom of God. He does this by hitting us where we are vulnerable. Anywhere there is a crack, he can enter. Has your home ever had insect problems? If so, you know all kinds of insects can take up residence inside your house through the smallest of cracks. When we moved into our home in Colorado, we found thousands of dead moths in the cracks of the gas fireplaces. They had entered through the small vents, which allow the gas fumes to get out. The pilot lights were not lit, as it was the middle of summer. The contractor who came to clean the fireplaces told us that if we keep the pilot lights lit year round, the moths won't come in, because they don't like the gas fumes. Simple, don't you think? If I choose not to keep the pilot lights lit, I am sending an invitation to the moths to come on in.

If we allow cracks in our faith, we are opening a door and sending an invitation to Satan to enter. How do we get cracks in our faith to begin with? Suppose you had a fight with your hubby last night. You were mad, he was mad, you exchanged words and then each left the room. The night went on; you kept to yourself in the bedroom while he stayed in his corner in the family room. You went to bed at separate times, slept, got up this morning, and then he left for work with no mention from either of you of the fight. Come on now, be honest; we have all done this. A simple situation like this is all it takes to start a crack. Any issue that creates space in our relationships is its beginning.

Just as your house requires constant sealing of cracks to keep insects and pests out, your heart needs continual guarding against invasion. How do you accomplish this? Don't let issues go unresolved. The longer you let things go, the harder they are to correct. This does not mean that you never disagree or fight with your family members, co-workers, or friends. There will always be disagreements; that is part of life. The way you respond to those situations is what makes the difference. Often, disagreements occur because of misinformation or miscommunication. Make sure you have your facts straight and have communicated them accurately to the other person. Sometimes, you have to agree to disagree. We are all human, and each of us is different from the other. You cannot always expect people to change to agree with what you think or want.

The key to success in securing our faith from invasion is making sure it is founded on the right source. If you place your faith in your spouse or your kids, you will be hurt. They are human and therefore incapable of meeting our every need. There is only one source upon which we can safely place all our faith and trust and feel completely confident that we will never be let down—God.

Let's revisit the confrontation I had with my daughter-in-law, Alison, over how she and Josh would spend block leave during his second deployment. I will paint the scene by reminding you that I am his mother and the one who gave birth to him. Therefore, I had every right to expect him to make time to spend with me on his leave. What do you notice about the last two sentences? It's all about me, my rights, and what I wanted. My feelings came from my thinking, but I did not have all the facts. I had not stopped to consider the viewpoint of the other person. I reacted to news and responded solely on the basis of my feelings, which were in turn based on faulty thinking. I was wrong! The point is, just because we think it and want it does not make it right.

I have a statement that I started using with my grandson, Noah. He is five and, as is true for most children that age, his perception is that the world is supposed to revolve around what he wants. When he starts down the "I want" path, I stop him and tell him to repeat after me: "I . . . don't . . . always . . . get . . . what . . . I . . . want." After hearing this a few times, he was onto me, and as soon as I would say, "Repeat after me," he would say, "Grandma, I don't like saying that."

We are like he is in this; we don't like it when we don't get what we want. As adults, though, we should have the ability to reason that the world does not revolve around our wants. We can grasp the need to stop and examine the entire situation before we respond to it.

Our faith in God comes from the knowledge that He alone is completely trustworthy. As we begin to trust Him and continue to do so, our faith grows and becomes a shield of protection. We cannot stop there. We must maintain the shield by preventing cracks. Occasionally, cracks will occur because we are not perfect. That is okay, but those cracks need attention. We must examine the cracks and determine what is required to seal them. We may need to revisit the situation that caused the crack, and we may need to seek forgiveness from God and perhaps someone else. Don't let doing nothing be an option. If you have a crack in your house and you do nothing, chances are the crack will get bigger. Bigger cracks invite larger invaders. Don't open your heart to unwanted guests. The only occupant of your heart should be your Lord and Savior, Jesus Christ.

Pick up that shield of faith.

S u m m a r y

- Get into an exercise program and keep physically fit. This will aid in keeping your mind sharp.

- Examine your faith closely. In whom or what are you placing your trust and hope? It should be God, because He is the only one who can meet your needs all the time.

- Look for cracks in your faith. Are there any unresolved issues hanging around? If so, resolve them. Do whatever you need to do to fix the cracks. This may require forgiving someone else, asking forgiveness from God and/or another, and forgiving yourself.

- Once you fix the cracks, seal up your faith by preventing new cracks. Pay close attention to how you respond to situations. Stop and think before you speak. Make sure you understand the entire situation. Take time to look at it from the perspective of the other person.

Prayer:

Heavenly Father,

Thank You for being the source of my faith. God, I ask You to help me examine my faith and open my eyes to any cracks or weaknesses in it. Father, I ask for the wisdom and understanding to correct any issues that need to be resolved.

Lord, help me to stop and think before I respond to situations in the future so that my response will align with Your will.

Father, thank You for Who You are and all that You do for me. Amen.

CHAPTER 19

Survival Skills

LET'S FACE IT, our sons and daughters are often in danger zones. They have risky jobs, and at any time, one of them could be seriously wounded. The military does a good job of equipping our service members with basic survival skills. Prior to deployment, they are trained to be first responders and can then take care of a wounded comrade or even themselves. This becomes second nature to them, and they respond without hesitation when a situation arises.

Last November while visiting Josh over Thanksgiving, I learned that he sprang into action at the scene of a traffic accident. The driver of a car had lost control; the vehicle rolled several times and ended up on its side in the grassy median strip. Josh witnessed the accident and noticed cars pulling over in front of him, alongside the Interstate. He decided to stop, and when he got out of his truck, he noticed the others who had pulled over were just standing beside their cars, looking at this vehicle in the median. He said he could hear a woman screaming from the car, so he immediately bolted down the slope toward the car. Both a man and a woman were trapped inside, and the woman's screams convinced Josh that she was panicking. He spotted a sunroof and told her to move away from it and cover her face. He kicked in the sunroof and then she was able to crawl through it or, as Josh described it, "She spilled through the hole." Josh turned his attention to the man still inside the car. He was bleeding badly from one arm, so Josh tore off a piece of the man's shirt, made a tourniquet and placed it on his upper arm. By this time, paramedics were arriving at the scene, so Josh departed. I was amazed when he returned to the house and told us this story. He hadn't thought about whether or not to help; his training kicked in and he sprang into action. Honestly, I would have been one of the people standing beside my car, looking on and wondering what to do.

We mothers need our own survival skills. At any time during our child's deployment, events can take a turn for the worse. We need to be prepared for any situation and be ready to spring into action immediately.

Do you recall Josh's first deployment? He was in Baghdad, and things were deteriorating there by the day. Civil unrest and war threatened to erupt right where he was serving. I was taking in every bit of news I could get in an effort to keep up with the events. At that time, I didn't realize that Josh was not the only one on the verge of war—so was I. The difference was, he was trained for his war; I was not. I did not have any survival skills. God met me there, and in the days and weeks that followed, He provided, through a Bible study, all the skills I would need. Not only did I survive war, I claimed victory.

We have examined the weapons and armor that God provides for us. Now I want to give you some practical things that you can do every day to stay strong and be ready for whatever comes up.

PRAY

Verse 18 of Ephesians 6 says, " . . . and pray in the Spirit on all occasions with all kinds of prayers and requests" (Ephesians 6:18, *NIV Study Bible*).

God does not tell us to pray because He needs to know what is going on with us. He already knows everything. God wants us to pray because it develops our trust in Him.

Think about your relationship with your husband. Do you talk to him? Imagine what it would be like if you never spoke to your husband.

In order for our spiritual relationship with God to grow, we need to talk to Him. If you are a person who is afraid to pray, remember that there is no wrong way to do it as long as you are speaking reverently from your heart. Praying is simply talking to God. You shouldn't worry about saying too much or not enough, because God knows everything you are thinking. I like talking to God throughout the day; it doesn't matter where I am or what I am doing. I can be in the shower, in my car, at work—it makes no difference. God is everywhere all the time, so I don't have to pray at a certain time, either. He is accessible anytime, anywhere.

I want to review a verse that I shared earlier about prayer:

> "Do not be anxious about anything, but in everything, by prayer and petition, with thanksgiving, present your requests to God. And the peace of God, which transcends all understanding, will guard your hearts and your minds in Christ Jesus". (Philippians 4:6,7, *NIV Study Bible*)

God instructs us to pray about everything, and when we do, His peace will guard our hearts and minds. That is why we pray.

Pray for the safety of your child. Pray for strength to endure each day. Pray for wisdom and guidance to deal with whatever today brings. Pray for faith to trust God more. Pray for everything.

FOCUS ON POSITIVES

It is very natural when dealing with a stressful situation to feel as if that ordeal is the only thing going on in your life. It's easy to lose sight of other happenings that may be positive. Conscious effort is needed to seek out the positives during a trial, but it is well worth the effort.

You may have encountered a situation like the one I am about to describe. I was having a bad day and admittedly feeling sorry for myself for a variety of reasons. At the grocery store, I saw a mother pushing a wheelchair of sorts. I say "of sorts" because it was not an ordinary wheelchair. The young child confined to the chair was severely disabled, and it seemed the chair completely encircled him. I felt guilty as I looked at the child and then at his mother. What was I pouting about? I stopped for a moment and tried to imagine what their every day must be like. I can't fathom the challenges they likely endure just to accomplish basic tasks. You don't have to look very far to find someone who is worse off than you.

Learn to count your blessings. Focus on all the things you have to be thankful for, instead of things that are not going as planned. A good exercise is to write down everything for which you are thankful. Post the list on your refrigerator and read it every morning. One thing I am so thankful for is that my son rose to the call of his nation and chose to serve. Yes, he has a dangerous job and the reality is that he could be wounded or killed. But it was his choice, and I am so proud of him for making it. If it weren't for the bravery of our sons and daughters, who would rise up to defend our great country? We know personally the sacrifices these brave men and women make as well as the sacrifices required of us. What an honor it is to know that your child was brave enough to answer that call. Focus on that.

REACH OUT TO OTHERS

Another common misconception that might assail you when in stressful situations is the feeling that you are the only one on the planet dealing with the issue at hand. This is never true, particularly for us as parents of service members. There are millions of service members in active and reserve status, currently serving, and they all have families somewhere.

When my son enlisted in the Army, I looked for a support group close to where I was at that time, in central Pennsylvania. There was none, not one. Nor did any church in my county provide support specific to military families. After I began writing this book, God gave me such a passion for military families that I wanted to do something to change the lack of support. I put together a proposal to start, in my church, a ministry that would focus on military families. Soon afterward, a family whose daughter had just joined the Marine Corp started coming to church. I saw prayer requests coming from this dear mom for the safety of her daughter and peace for the family. My heart broke for her, knowing exactly how she felt and, in addition, considering the added fear and concern she must have with a daughter serving. I reached out to this woman, Paula, and invited her to lunch. I shared with her my passion for military families and asked if she would join me in launching this ministry. She was thrilled at the opportunity, and we proceeded to get approval from the Board of Elders. We launched Military Families Ministry at the State College Alliance Church in State College, Pennsylvania, in January of 2010. There we created a hero board where we displayed pictures of service members who were in some way connected to our church. We started an Adopt a Service Member program, where people in the congregation could sign up to "adopt" one of our heroes. They would commit to pray for the service member and his or her family and send cards and care packages. We were able to minister in this way to the eleven service members connected to our church. But ours was just one church, in one county, in one state. There are so many more service members who need support.

As of this writing, Paula is leading this seminal ministry group at the church in Pennsylvania. As I mentioned earlier my husband, Jeff, and I relocated to Colorado this year due to a change in his work. When I shared the news about our move with Paula, I remember telling her, "I don't get it, all this planning and preparation to launch this ministry, we finally do it, and now I have to leave." Paula replied, "This was just your training. God is going to use this ground work to start this ministry in new places." How amazing is our God? I have launched a second Military Families Ministry group at the Mountain View Fellowship Church in Strasburg, Colorado. We have our own hero board, which displays 21 service members, all of whom will be adopted by a family in our congregation. Both groups have knitters making prayer patches and prayer shawls to give to our heroes and their families. We've recruited schools and other organizations in these communities to join us by writing letters and cards, donating items for care packages, and partnering up for community events to honor and support military families.

Please don't sit at home and think you are all alone. You are not. God is with you always, and if you get out and look around you will find others who are dealing with the same thing you are. Use that. Go get connected and do something. One of the best things you can do to take your mind off your situation is help someone else with circumstances they are facing.

REMEMBER, IT'S PERSISTENCE—NOT PERFECTION

Whatever you do, keep in mind that it is not about being perfect at anything. God knows we are not capable of perfection. All we can do is be persistent in the things God is calling us to do. Expect hurdles and disappointments along the way; they are part of life. Learn something from each hurdle and keep on moving. If things were perfect all the time, if everything worked out exactly the way we planned it, what would we learn? I certainly did not plan to set up a new ministry and then be transplanted across the country. God, however, had a different plan for me and I trust Him. I know that God's plan for my life is better than anything I could imagine.

KEEP IN TOUCH

When your child deploys, one of the toughest things to endure is the lack of communication. Depending upon where your service member is, communication may be limited. Many times, phones for soldiers' use are scarce and must be shared. Internet availability is hit or miss, and if our soldier does get a good connection, it may happen when we are sleeping, due to the time difference. In addition to these issues, if your child is married, he or she will likely be calling the spouse more frequently than phoning you. Remind yourself that spouses deserve priority. Support them.

Be creative about keeping in touch with your child. Don't think that the only time to communicate is when he or she contacts you. That is simply not true. You can initiate communication as often as you want. Our service members appreciate receiving things from us and knowing we are thinking about them and praying for them. Send them cards for no reason at all, other than to let them know you are thinking about them. Send them packages with their favorite snacks and other things they may not be able to get where they are.

If your child is married, stay in touch with his or her spouse. Put yourself in their shoes and try to understand the sacrifice they are enduring, as well. If you focus your energies on supporting your child's spouse as much as you can, you will find compassion for that in-law child and realize that the two of you want the same thing. You both want your son or daughter, their husband or wife, to stay safe and return home as soon as possible. Don't forget that we are the parents, we are older and wiser, and we are responsible for being mentors and supporters for our kids and their spouses. Don't fight with them; love and encourage them.

Summary

- Pray, pray, pray. Pray about everything. Trust God to hear and answer your prayers.

- Focus on positives. Look around you and make a list of all the things you have to be thankful for. Volunteer at a shelter or help someone less fortunate than you.

- Reach out to others in your situation; get connected. Find other military families in your community and start a support group. Visit my website at www.militaryfamiliesministry.com to see how you can get involved with our ministry.

- Quit trying to be perfect; focus on being persistent. Set a goal and keep working toward it until you get it done.

- Keep in touch with your service member any way you can. If your child is married, love and support his or her spouse.

Prayer:

Father God,

Thank You for being so faithful in meeting my every need. Lord, open my eyes to see opportunities that You place before me. Lead me to people who are enduring the same situation that I am. Help me to minister to those less fortunate than I and to be aware of how You have blessed my life.

Father, expand my heart to reach out to my child and his or her spouse. Help me to see them and love them as You do. Teach me new things through this experience, that I may grow in faith. Amen.

CHAPTER 20

Post-Traumatic Stress Disorder

I AM NOT going to pretend to be an expert on PTSD. In fact, I will tell you that I have received no formal training whatsoever. What I know about this subject is purely from my own research into the disorder. PTSD is a serious issue that affects many military families, and it is something we must address.

If you think for a moment about some of the things our service members see and do while deployed, it is not hard to understand why they come home traumatized. The frequency of deployments during war times, further complicates this issue, as they barely have time to recover from a deployment before they are sent back to a war zone. In addition to the issues they physically encounter on deployments, there are difficulties that arise from being away from their families for extended periods. They can't just flip a switch, turn off war mode and enter civilian life. Reintegration takes time, and the adjustment is a challenge for the whole family.

The various branches of the armed forces do what they can to reach out to and counsel service members who are affected, but it is not enough. Staff and funding are limited. They are now hiring civilian counselors who are certified in dealing with PTSD. It is still not enough.

At the same time, many soldiers do not seek help with this syndrome for fear of repercussions from unit members or commanders. No one wants to appear to be weak, so they suck it up and pretend nothing is wrong. While this may work for a while, the long-term effects of suppressing these feelings are devastating.

We are mothers of these soldiers and we need to be pro-active with PTSD. No one knows the normal behavior of our child better than we do. We need to research and learn the warning signs of PTSD. Pay attention when your son or daughter returns from deployment. If you are not living in the same house as your child, it may be difficult to pick up on little things that just don't seem right. If you child is married, talk to his or her spouse and ask the tough questions. How are they adjusting to their life back home? Do they seem normal? Are they agitated easily? Talk to your child; ask how he is doing, if he is having nightmares. Don't be afraid to bring things up. Try to get your child talking about experiences while on deployment. If he feels safe talking to someone (like you, his mom), he will likely open up. Early intervention is critical to successfully treating PTSD.

When service members return home from deployments, there are certain behaviors that are simply part of adjusting to life back home. It is important to be aware of these and understand that they should be temporary.

Some of these behaviors are:

- Impatience with our trivial, everyday dramas. Remember, your child has been dealing with life or death situations for the past year, so allow time for adjustment to normal life.

- Nightmares may be common for a while. If these don't cease, your son or daughter may need help.

- Jumpiness at bangs or loud noises, reminiscent of gunfire, is common. This, too, should pass in time.

The following may be normal adjustment behaviors for a period of time but, if they continue, may be signs of PTSD:

- Frequent nightmares

- Inability to focus

- Inability to sleep

- Replaying or flashbacks of a traumatic event

- Physical changes such as rapid heart rate and or sweating when thoughts of the event occur

- Loss of interest in activities that are normally enjoyed

- Frequent agitation or outbursts of anger

- Drug or alcohol abuse. This warrants immediate attention.

This is not a complete list of the symptoms of PTSD, nor does a service member need to display all of these symptoms to be diagnosed with it. The key is be alert; pay attention to the behaviors of your child upon return home. If you sense something is not right, ask your child if he or she noticed it as well. If denial or defensiveness is the response when you bring it up, you may need to seek help from a professional. Your concern is reason enough to seek advice.

The rate of suicide among service members is growing at an alarming rate. The rate of spousal abuse involving returning soldiers is also on the rise.

As the mother of a service member, I urge you to do your own research on the topic of PTSD, learn all the symptoms and treatment options. Trust your instincts when your child returns home, and don't be afraid to raise the issue with your child and his or her spouse.

Chapter 21

Graduation

CONGRATULATIONS! You've made it to the end of boot camp, and today is your graduation day.

You may be waiting for or have just attended your child's graduation from basic training. It is an amazing day, filled with mixed emotions. There is so much pride in our new service member and the noticeable changes in him or her. We anxiously await the next step. We wonder where he or she will go and how soon deployment will come. Alternatively, perhaps, you are a seasoned military mom and have already "served out deployments" with your child. Regardless of how long you have been involved, I pray you feel better equipped for the journey that lies ahead.

Keep in mind the fact that your child has been trained by the best. Regardless of the branch in which he or she serves, your child has undergone the most extensive military training in the world and is ready for whatever will come next. Our armed forces carry their training with them.

The question is, will you? Will you carry this training with you as you journey through your child's first or next deployment? Remember, it is a choice—your choice. You can use this information and suit up daily, or you can stand this book on a shelf and forget about it. I ask you to examine your heart and soul today. I ask you to do what you expect your child to do. Use your training, be safe, be smart, and be prepared for whatever your future holds.

It is my hope and prayer that knowing my story will help you navigate your own path. Perhaps the lessons I've learned through my son's two deployments will serve as a strong starting point. As you work your way through your child's deployments, you will learn your own lessons. I pray that you will use each lesson as an opportunity to grow closer to your Lord and Savior.

I offer the following prayer for you.

Heavenly Father,

Thank You for Your faithfulness to the reader of this book, I pray, Father, that You will touch this individual and guide her life. I ask You to bless this person and her entire family. Lord, I ask for Your protection over her loved one as he or she serves in our military. I pray You will bring peace that transcends all understanding to this family when their child is deployed. Draw them close to You and use their experience to elevate them to a new spiritual maturity.

Lord, thank You for who You are and for all that You do for us every day. Amen.

End Notes

1   Neil T. Anderson, Breaking Through to Spiritual Maturity (Ventura, CA: Gospel Light, 2000), p.59. All references used by permission.
2   *Ibid,* p.59.
3   *Ibid,* p.59.
4   *Ibid*, p.69.
5   *Ibid*, p.69.
6   *Ibid*, p.76.
7   *Ibid*, p. 151.
8   *Ibid*, p. 151.
9   *Ibid*, p. 151.
10 Rescue, Written by Jared Anderson (Vertical Worship Songs ASCAP 2003)

ABOUT THE AUTHOR

Tracie Ciambotti is the co-founder of Military Families Ministry, a non-profit group that supports service members and their families. Her experiences as the mother of an Army infantryman over the past six years have afforded her the passion and knowledge to be an advocate for military families. Tracie is a contributor to the blog, "Off The Base", which focuses on creating civilian awareness of military life.

Tracie lives in Bennett, Colorado, with her husband, Jeff. Tracie is a conference speaker and has led Bible study groups for more than five years. She writes short stories for a local publication and produces a newsletter for Military Families Ministry.

Made in the USA
Middletown, DE
18 January 2022

59044675R00073